DIED TWICE !

YET STILL VERY MUCH ALIVE AND KICKING

A compilation of quasi articulate unauthorized autobiographical ramblings.

Bernard D. Shapiro

First published by Dog Ear Publishing
4010 W. 86th Street, Ste H
Indianapolis, IN 46268
www.dogearpublishing.net

ISBN: 978-1-4575-1866-9

This book is printed on acid-free paper.

Printed in the United States of America

DEDICATION

This compilation of enduring life experiences is dedicated with tender compassion to my only son Marc Jeffrey Shapiro who, regretfully, has spent the last forty six years incapacitated, in a wheel chair, requiring everlasting care for his basic needs.

It is often said that losing a child is one of the most agonizing traumas a parent can endure. Having him disabled these many years, both mentally and physically, has assuredly exacerbated my torment, and no doubt more consequentially, his.

Mercifully, I have been able to "move on," but unfortunately he has not.

May God be eternally gentle with his soul.

Amen!!

Marc Jeffrey Shapiro-Sept.1967

ACKNOWLEDGEMENTS

I would be remiss if I did not offer my undying thanks to those three hundred selfless human beings that volunteered to "Pattern"* my son in 1968/69.

Their dedication was truly astounding, as there was never a time that we did not have a full complement of five qualified volunteers present and accounted for. They are too numerous to mention here, but those that participated know who they are, and I hope they accept my eternal gratitude for their assistance in my hour of need.

Additionally, I also wish to acknowledge those who were so supportive of me in 2010 when Laura passed unexpectedly under bizarre circumstances.

I owe particular appreciation to our friends, the Birnbaums, Lessers, and Mederricks, all of who had their own special relationship with Laura; as each of these couples have gone out of their way to "be there" during my immediate grieving, and for the ensuing three years. In addition, my dear friend Paul Shapiro was by my side when I needed him the most, every day for the first two months after Laura passed.

I also pay very precious homage to Martha Kraska in her dual role as Granny and *Nana*. Her extraordinary dedication (with the support of her husband Peter), in caring for Marley and Luca has been unwavering and of profound consolation to me ever since *Nana* passed. I am so thankful the children will have such a nurturing grandmother as they mature.

To have all those caring people be supportive on two separate occasions, some forty two years apart, is something I shall always remember and cherish.

THANK YOU ————AND GOD BLESS YOU ALL

* Patterning: a non medically accepted, physically intensive, rehabilitative regimen, for those individuals who have suffered extensive neurological brain damage.

TABLE OF CONTENTS

INTRODUCTION

On April 29th, 2010 my life as I knew it ended........ for the second time.

Forty three years earlier, in October of 1967, I "lost" my five year old son to an accident in which he suffered life threatening injuries. After colliding with his older sister's school bus while riding his bicycle, he suffered severe brain damage that ensured he would never again be able to function as a normal child, and to this day at the age of fifty, he remains incapacitated, requiring perpetual care and support.

That was the very first time "I died," and for these last forty six years I have strived to rebuild my life. I truly believed I was doing a credible job until I "died" again, for the second time, when my wife of thirty nine years passed away suddenly, under bizarre circumstances, without ever having been ill.

Officially, the autopsy report indicated that she died of heart failure just as she was being prepped to undergo a laser surgical procedure. Painfully, we will never know definitively what caused her heart to surrender; a reality that has been extremely difficult for my family to deal with, but lacking any meaningful alternative, we have come to accept that sometimes god works in mysterious ways.

Knowing that I am not alone in having experienced life altering tragedies, nor the only person that has managed to successfully "soldier on," I have neither sought nor required sympathy, when either of these two unrelated incidents, forty three years apart, dramatically affected my life. I do, however, fervently thank all those caring souls who supported me in my times of need.

Those that know me now, can hopefully understand how those two tragedies greatly affected my life, my character and my perspective. I know I have matured and gained wisdom from both life altering occurrences, and I have managed "to move on," and what follows is a disjointed abridged outline of my life story as best I can recount it.

I ask the reader to graciously allow me a degree of poetic license as to dates and sequence of events, as all this has been written strictly from the memory of a seventy seven year old " puppy" who is still young at heart and "wagging his tail."

Since I concluded that many of the experiences were not appropriate to work into the initial narrative, I have chosen to chronicle a series of detailed addendums and post scripts, some quite brief and others somewhat lengthy, and hopefully you will take the time to read them in order to understand "the whole enchilada."

Whereas I performed my own editing and copywriting, I take full responsibility for any spelling or grammatical errors. Hopefully, they will not exist or that you will either not notice them or will diplomatically overlook them, as you will be focused on the narrative itself.

I recognize that for much of what I have written, you "had to be there" to fully appreciate the moments and situations that I found myself in over the years; some tragic, some serious, and some humorous.

As an artist might do, I have attempted to "paint a picture" for all to see.

How it is viewed and interpreted will be up to you the reader.

"DYING" THE FIRST TIME !!! 1967-1970

In early October, 1967, my son Marc Jeffery Shapiro, a very athletic and active five year old, returned home from school and found his way down the steps to our basement and into the garage to his newly gifted two-wheeler. He then managed to activate the automatic garage door and proceeded to ride his bike down our inclined driveway, knowing full well that he was not allowed to do that unless either I or his mother were with him. I was in NYC at work and my wife of eight years was in NYC on what she said later was a shopping trip. The housekeeper had just given him his milk and cookies when he "disappeared" down the stairs and before she noticed he was gone, he was on his bike heading down the driveway.

Unfortunately, his sister's school bus was coming down Tara Drive, and Marc slammed into the bus that was screeching to a halt. He was thrown backwards on to the grass, but his head hit a fire hydrant and rendered him unconscious, and he remained in that condition until he arrived via ambulance at North Shore Hospital in Manhasset.

I shall never forget the frantic phone call I received in my office from one of my neighbors telling me that Marc had been hit and was being rushed to the hospital. I graphically recall racing out of my office and onto 5th Ave. and hailing a taxi and directing him to the Mid Town tunnel and out to Long Island, not knowing if my son was alive or dead.

Upon arriving at the hospital emergency room I was directed to the surgical waiting room where I was told the doctors would be out shortly to speak to me. After what seemed like an eternity, two neurosurgical residents entered and informed me that although Marc was alive, he was critical and suffering from extreme edema of the brain, a condition that precluded them from any remedial action until the swelling abated. They also informed me that although there was a medication that would help in relieving the swelling, it was not available at the hospital at that moment and they questioned the wisdom of pursuing this course of action.

They explained that even if the serum was located and administered, the amount of time that Marc's brain had been oxygen deprived would more than likely render him permanently disabled with his brain pretty much staying at the level of a two year old for the rest of his life, and if he was just left unmedicated, the seriousness of the swelling would probably mercifully claim his life. That was truly the first time in my life ……….. "I died."

I was alone in the surgical waiting room with a decision to make; my wife some-where in NYC but unreachable. Did I "die" right then and there having lost my son, or was I to fight for his life and secure the medication and try to defy the future laid out for him by the doctors?

The decision was instantaneous, as I could not "die" having another child at home and one on the way, so I had to live for my family and as a father I had to do every-thing possible to save my son and fight for any future he might have. There was really no option!!! I had momentarily "died" but kept on breathing.

After a few frenzied phone calls, and frantic pleading, the medication was located in NYC and a friend of mine with hospital connections, managed to have the anti inflammatory serum rushed out from the city and it was then immediately admin-istered to my son, resulting in the swelling being reduced and his life being spared.

Hours later, my wife was escorted to the hospital to hear the devastating news directly from me. I never left the hospital that day and ended up "living there" for the next three days, using the hospital facilities for my basic needs, with neighbors or my wife bringing me fresh clothes.

Three weeks later, Marc was released from the intensive care unit. He then spent four months in a private room at North Shore Hospital in a coma as a result of the oxygen deprivation and seriousness of his injuries.

My life had been instantly altered and my entire focus was on Marc's recovery. In the ensuing months, with the help of my sympathetic car pool neighbors, I stopped at the hospital every morning on the way to work and every evening on the way home. My wife visited during the day with the support of her girl friends, and to all those com-passionate people I will be eternally grateful.

During the ensuing four months, we were able to survive the daily trauma due to the warmth and tenderness of the nursing staff and particularly the pediatric nurs-ing supervisor who made things as comfortable for us as possible. It was during those months that both my wife and I developed a true friendship with this young lady who possessed a genuine nursing persona. *Little did I know that four years later this compassionate supervisor and I would become romantically involved, and eventually married.*

In February of 1968, I was informed by a hospital administrator that since Marc was now out of his coma, I would have to arrange for his release from the hospital as it was not a long term care facility and they needed his room for other patients. My wife Toby was upstairs in the maternity ward giving birth to my daughter Elissa and my son was on the first floor, alive and out of his coma, but totally incapacitated and unable to communicate.

And so began the task of rebuilding of my life, as I was dedicated to having Marc make as full of a recovery as humanly possible.

After extensive research I contacted Blythedale Children's Hospital in Valhalla N.Y as they had an outstanding reputation for rehabilitation work with brain injured children. Marc was accepted for a two month trial for both physical and speech therapy. During this period, I picked him up every Friday afternoon and brought him home to my family in Roslyn, returning him on Sunday evening for his five day Monday to Friday rehabilitation regimen. Unfortunately, at the end of the two months, the hospital advised us that Marc was not making any progress and their prognosis was crushing as they suggested that he be placed in a 24/7 full care facility.

I stubbornly refused to give up fighting for Marc's recovery, so I then transported him to the Patterning Center in Media Pennsylvania, where they offered a last resort, non medically approved program for resurrecting his damaged nervous system and re educating his muscles and brain. This was an excruciatingly physical rehabilitation regimen, requiring two hundred and eighty volunteers a week to visit our Roslyn home as the patterning therapy consisted of special hourly body movement of Marc's extremities, necessitating a five man team working in unison for forty five minutes, manipulating his arms, legs and head in a very precise manner.

That eight hour regimen required forty volunteers daily, with twenty substitutes on a standby basis. I hired a secretary, installed a special phone line, and organized the three hundred people all of whom would either show up at the appointed hour or call in advance to advise of their unavailability, and the secretary would then arrange for one of the standby volunteers to fill in. I found myself forever grateful to these people who willingly gave of their time and effort every day for over a year.

You can imagine the stress this placed on my family, with my seven year old daughter Lauren, having initially witnessed her brother slamming in to her school bus, and then visiting him in the hospital and now experiencing all that was going on around her, with my wife having just given birth to our third child and the enormity of having almost three hundred volunteers come to our home weekly. After a year of grueling patterning I had to finally accept the irrefutable fact that Marc's brain damage was irreversible, and indeed he did need to be placed in an appropriate full care facility. Fortunately, soon thereafter, he was accepted at the Suffolk State School on Long Island, just about ½ hour from our home. The experience of visiting him there was heartbreaking for me as I was exposed to a part of life that thankfully most people never witness; and that is the amount of incapacitated people that are in need of 24/7 care, either emotionally, physically or mentally. Thankfully, shortly thereafter, we were able to have Marc transferred to a New York State sponsored residential facility located in Malvern, where he has resided all these years with nine other handicapped "boys and girls," with Marc having lived there the longest.

The endless trauma created by all of this activity, exacerbated what was a most difficult situation and eventually led to the dissolution of my first marriage which was already on rocky grounds prior to the accident. There was no way I would address the marriage difficulties until I ensured that Marc was properly situated and well cared for. Once that was accomplished, I was able to confront my wife about her extra marital affair and demanded a divorce. At first she was willing to give me custody of our two daughters, then 8 and 1, but reneged on that agreement upon the urgings of her mother and sister, who convinced her to maintain custody lest she be thought of as an uncaring mother. She did however agree to move out of the marital home, as she did not want anyone to become aware of her adulterous behavior. The quid pro quo being that I would keep her escapades private.

Upon our divorce, she, my two daughters, and our live-in housekeeper, all moved into a three bedroom apartment in Forest Hills. After a month, I received a frantic phone call from my daughter Lauren saying she was in trouble with the building's superintendent, as she had just "crayoned" the hallway. When I asked to speak to Toby she informed me that her mother was in Puerto Rico, and she and her sister were alone with the house keeper, but she was not allowed to tell anyone that.

There I was working in my showroom with Neiman Marcus in mid afternoon and my daughter was on the phone hysterical. Not knowing exactly what to do, I called Laura Martin, the pediatric supervisor that had been so helpful to us with Marc, as I knew she lived in Flushing fairly close to the children and that her shift would be soon be over. I asked her if she could possibly run over and help out with the situation.

Laura, who had developed a close friendship with my wife, was shocked to learn that the children were left in the care of the housekeeper as Toby was out of the country. She too, was upset with her for not at least giving her a "heads up."

A month later, my wife was remarried and advised me she was moving to Puerto Rico with the children, as her new husband was a lawyer with a New York firm but assigned to their San Juan office for two years.

I fought that legally, and tried to obtain custody of the girls, as my separation and divorce agreements precluded Toby from moving more than fifty miles from New York City with the children. The judge, however, ruled in Toby's favor as she was now "legitimately married to an attorney," and he felt that ruling was in the best interest of the children.

In the matter of less than two years, I had "lost" my son, was divorced, and my two daughters were ferreted out of the country and I found myself at the ripe old age of thirty three, understandably distraught and alone.

****

In retrospect, on the brighter and lighter side, it was perhaps the shortest alimony obligation on record. I try to laugh every day at life itself, and I do believe god works in strange ways.

FORTY YEARS OF LIVING 1970-2010

Shortly thereafter, I asked Laura to join me for dinner one evening to thank her for all that she had done over the prior three years, as I knew she herself was experiencing the pain of a divorce from her relatively short marriage. Over the course of a few months our friendship grew and eventually developed into a romance and we were married in the spring of 1971, and that was the start of my "moving on."

It was March 26th that Laura and I unceremoniously found our way to City Hall, where we were wed by a Justice of the Peace, with her nursing friend Margaret as our sole witness. The three of us then taxied uptown to the St. Regis Hotel, where sitting next to Salvatore Dali, we had our celebratory luncheon and then, and only then, did we mail our wedding announcement cards to friends and family. That evening our parents and her grandmother joined us for our "wedding dinner" at the Pierre Hotel. So we would always say,
"We had a Pierre wedding… minus a few of the trappings."

We then took up residence in my 35th St. apartment on Lexington Ave. in NYC, and Laura reverse commuted to North Shore Hospital, where she was now the head nurse in their newly opened radiology department.

We planned two honeymoons. The first one a week after our marriage, when we flew down to Puerto Rico and picked up my daughters Lauren (10), and Elissa (3) and flew over to St. Thomas where we chartered a 46 foot houseboat that I was to navigate thru the American & British Virgin Islands.

Laura had agreed to this, in spite of the fact that she could not swim and we would be bearing the responsibility of my three year old, but we did just fine and had a marvelous time, cruising, swimming, snorkeling, and sun bathing. To this day, it was one of the most enjoyable weeks I have ever spent on the water. Additionally, it gave the four of us a chance "to bond" as we were all starting new lives and I desperately wanted my two daughters to share fun times with us.

Three weeks later, Laura and I left for a ten day jaunt to London, Paris, and Rome as this was part of the honeymoon deal we had made. Since it was to be Laura's first exposure to Europe, we were both quite excited.

Our trip ended in Naples and from there down to Torre del Greco which at the time was the coral capitol of the world and the home, museum, and work shop of the

Italian coral king, Mr. Basilio Liverino. Willingly, he shared with us his vast knowledge of coral and its potential applicability to fashion jewelry. I can proudly and honestly say that this connection greatly advanced the semi precious phase of the fashion jewelry business as it exits in America today.

To put things in chronological perspective for you, while still married to Toby, and before Marc's accident, I had started my fashion jewelry company, Les Bernard Inc. in 1963 with my partner Lester Joy and the financial aid and wisdom of my dad, who was well known and highly respected in the fashion jewelry industry.

With their expertise and participation, Les Bernard quickly became an important contributor to the upscale fashion jewelry industry, with a national advertising campaign that was featured in the New Yorker, Vogue, Harpers, Elle, and the New York Sunday Times magazine section. It was truly a spirited campaign that lasted some twenty five years from 1965 to 1990.

Our very creative and well made fashion jewelry soon established an industry standard that was featured in hundreds of local upscale retailer newspaper ads that ran nationwide, and after fifteen years, we had well over two thousand retail outlets, both large and small, in just about every State.

We were known for our innovative products which were quickly "adapted" by other manufacturers in the industry. We were especially renowned for our "diamonds by the yard," baby chains, moveable flower pins, genuine marcasite on gold plate, 14 karat gold plated " diamond pointed" sterling silver pins and rings, and of course, eventually most well known for our introduction of semi precious materials to the fashion jewelry industry.

In 1971, a month after our honeymoon and our trip to Naples, our coral cache of fifty or so pieces was sold out. This prompted me to plan another quick trip to Naples, where we purchased a few hundred strands of Mr. Liverino's Mediterranean coral in red, orange, white and angel skin pink hues.

Those pieces also sold out in a very brief period, indicating to me that there was indeed a need for semi precious gems within the fashion jewelry industry. Hence was born the travel odyssey that Laura and I shared over the following twenty five years.

We returned to Europe in 1972 and 1973, seeking not only coral, but also from Idar Oberstein, Germany, tiger eye, rose quartz, sodalite, aventurine, tourmaline, peridot and amber, not only in finished strands, but also in loose beads or buttons. From there, we started to build the very unique Les Bernard collection of "rare species" fashion gems that we became nationally identified with for the next twenty years.

Laura and I moved to a home on Long Island in 1973, but continued to travel at least twice a year to Europe, seeking new ideas and "undiscovered" semi- precious raw materials to be manipulated in Les Bernard's New York state of the art manufacturing facility.

In the summer of 1974 my head designer and I flew to Montreal to a trade show featuring products from Mainland China, fully aware that at that time we were not permitted to either visit Mainland China or engage there in commerce, but rather only with The Republic of China, known to us as Taiwan. I was just very curious to see what mysterious "hidden gems" we were missing out on.

At the show we met an influential Chinese lady residing in Hong Kong, who informed us that the U. S. was conducting talks with the Mainland and that soon we would be able to trade with China and she promised, upon that happening, she would make sure that Les Bernard was invited to visit and do business. We kind of shrugged that off as we did not anticipate much progress in that area, but much to our pleasant surprise, shortly thereafter, President Nixon "opened up" Mainland China to American trade and travel.

After returning from our semi annual European buying trip, I arrived at my desk to find an invitation to the 1974 October Canton (now Kwangchow) Trade Fair that featured all of the products I had previously seen in Montreal, which not only included semi precious materials, but cloisonné jewelry as well.

Laura asked me, "how can we go to China now, as we have just returned from 10 days in Europe?" My response was, "How can we not go?" And off we went, and consequentially Les Bernard was the first fashion jewelry company to do business with the Mainland. That was the beginning of our two dozen Asian trips that spanned the years of 1974-1995 and included not only Mainland China, but also Taiwan, the Philippines, Japan, Thailand, India, and of course the most important of all Hong Kong.

Although I had "died" back in 1967, and divorced in 1969, I managed to "keep on breathing," re married in 1971 and had two more daughters, Blair on November 30th, 1973 and Brie on July 1, 1975, and was nurturing a growing fashion jewelry business.

The semi precious collection was so successful that we continued our numerous buying trips thru 1990. However, sensing a growing demand for our fashion styling from some European retailers, I decided to join the Providence Jewelers Association early on with a display at the Basel Fair in the early 1980's. I must say this was a fairly bold maneuver as almost all the other exhibitors were in the fine jewelry business selling gold and diamonds and precious stones.

We found ourselves in the company of Henry Dunay, and Jose Hess among other well-known jewelry designers, which was a little intimidating at first, but after a day or two I realized that my instincts were "right on" as there was a demand among upscale European retailers for our fashion jewelry as well. We then started traveling to every European fashion trade show that I thought appropriate for the Les Bernard collection and soon found ourselves in Paris, Madrid, Milan, Hong Kong, Düsseldorf & Frankfurt. Every show had a twice a year exhibition, so we "were on the road" quite a bit, both buying raw materials and then selling our American made jewelry abroad. We also travelled to Hamburg, London, Lisbon, and Stuttgart where we "set up" in the hotels and the local retailers who could not make the shows, came to buy from us in private showings.

I would have to say that this amount of international travel was a very important part of my second life and marriage, especially since we managed to take Blair and Brie with us on numerous trips and exposed them early on to different cultures and whetted their "travel appetites."

By 1990, many of our domestic retailers had closed their doors and our newly established international business helped us thru some very difficult seasons. Europe became our biggest single territory, which I know did not sit well with my domestic sales staff, but it was what it was and I was always grateful we had a growing business overseas while the domestic market for fashion jewelry was undergoing both the shrinkage of our better retailers and the advent of the minimalist look that pervaded the fashion industry at that time.

In 1991, I sold Les Bernard to a Providence manufacturer who asked that I stay on for five years as their international sales representative, so our travel continued until 1996, peaking with nine international trade shows in 1992 which had us on a plane every six weeks.

At the conclusion of my contract, my affiliation with my former company ceased and I retired from the fashion jewelry business.

While living our normal family life back in Muttontown, raising two lovely daughters, Laura and I had managed to visit over eighty major cities in twenty four countries with numerous overseas international trips over a twenty five year time span. Additionally, my visits to my regional showrooms and personal appearances at well known U. S. retail outlets led us to thirty three cities in twenty eight states.

I reiterate that in addition to the comfortable life style my business afforded us, our traveling was by far the most rewarding part of our life's journey as Laura managed to make almost every single trip with me, and it was a cherished twenty-five year bonding adventure.

After retiring from the fashion industry, I enjoyed brief stints as a yacht salesman, an owner of a small local landscape company, a consultant to and then superintendent of the Muttontown building department and then eventually as the Village Administrator.

During those 'non travelling years" we purchased a water front site in French St. Martin and built a home that we all enjoyed from 2000 to 2010, at which point we sold it and bought property in Costa Rica.

We had our fill of international travel and were happy to just fly between New York and our Caribbean paradise for those ten years.

Building another dream house in Costa Rica never happened as on April 29th, 2010, I "died" again when Laura was taken from us under shocking circumstances. She was never sick, but experienced heart failure as she was about to have laser surgery for a kidney stone.

Blair and I drove her to St. Francis hospital in the late afternoon of April 28th where she was admitted to the emergency room for an overnight stay prior to her scheduled surgery. Both girls then spent the evening at her side laughing and trying to make the best of the situation. The next morning when I went to keep her company I could tell she was in distress and things spiraled dramatically downward quite rapidly. She was rushed to the operating room for her scheduled surgery and the next thing we knew she had succumbed to heart failure. What a shock to all three of us, as we were expecting to take her home that very afternoon after she was released. She never made it out of the operating room in spite of the fact that the entire St. Francis emergency cardiac staff worked on her for three hours, reviving her five times.

Once again, a loved one was snatched from me, and once again my life was significantly altered in a matter of moments. Once again, I had to make a decision to "soldier on" as now I had two other daughters and two lovely grand children and I had to "hang around" for them.

So, although I had "died twice," I have kept on breathing and have now entered another phase of my adult life.

A MORE DETAILED OVERVIEW 1936- 2010

Now that you have read a brief overview of the last fifty years, I will, in the remaining pages, proceed to fill in additional details as they relate to some of my meaningful experiences.

The first twenty two years of my life were filled with school, friends, and athletics and all the usual suspects. I was born in the Bronx on March 30, 1936 and shared a bedroom with my maternal grandfather with whom I communicated solely in Yiddish. Yes, I was fluent at three, but can not utter a word today as he eventually remarried and moved out to an upstate farm that I often heard about, but never was privileged to visit.

In 1941 we moved to Rego Park in Queens where I attended PS. 139, Halsey Jr. High, & finally, Forest Hills High School which I graduated from in 1953. From the time I was eight, I was a worker, earning seasonal money by shoveling snow from driveways, and then at nine, I became the Saturday morning delivery boy for the Carolina Hand Laundry that serviced the area, and I made about $5 in tips for six hours work.

When I was twelve my parents rented a one bedroom apartment in Long Beach, a block from the ocean. and it did not take me long to land a job as a delivery boy in the deli of the nearby President Hotel. That first summer, I was one of four young men working there, but I soon became the sole survivor, working the counter, handling the stocking of the shelves and still delivering. Seven days a week, I reported at 7 AM and my day was over by 2 PM when I joined my friends on the beach.

I worked every summer there until I finished my freshman year in college, and my dad said, "It is time to get a real job," and he "recruited me" into his jewelry firm which required commuting to NYC.

My childhood, as I knew it, was indeed over.

As a high school teenager, I was definitely into sports and not a great social mixer. In fact, if the truth is to be told, I was extremely shy with the ladies, a trait that lasted until I was uncorked some sixty years later.

Due to a coach's strike during my sophomore and junior high school years, there were no extra curricular activities, so my competitive swimming experience was brief, but I did earn a Varsity Letter and a jacket, but that in itself is quite a story which I detail in the addendum section.

When I graduated Forest Hills High School, I was a better than average student and I had a respectable 88% average which surly was enough to allow me to be the first one in my family to attend college. Of course, I aimed high as my high school adviser never made me aware of two things.

Firstly, he neglected to tell me that I was applying to only very difficult schools to get into, and secondly that I should have a "safe school" if needed. What did I know? I applied to Cornell, Colgate, Brown, Union, and Bowdoin, and was summarily rejected at all five. I then scurried to apply to Queens College and the University of Wisconsin in Madison as "safe schools." I was accepted at those two institutions, but I had no desire to either remain at home while attending school or to attend an impersonal large university. It was not until the late Spring of 1953 that thru a friend of my parents, I applied to Clark University in Worcester, Mass.

Clark was a very small liberal arts school that was well regarded in academic circles, but enjoyed little public recognition. I went up for an interview, and was accepted and matriculated for the class of 57' and it turned out to be a perfect place for me to be; small in both physical plant, and population, and warm and personal.

Four years later, I graduated cum laude, Phi Beta Kappa, with honors in Government and International Relations, and a member of Gryphon, the senior men's honorary society, a dual distinction, never previously achieved. I ended up with a 3.85 GPA and was co editor in chief of the weekly school newspaper, a member of the JV basketball team, the manager of the varsity baseball team and an Inter Fraternity Council member, and profiled in the 1957 edition of "Who's Who" in American Colleges and Universities. For laughs "and revenge," I always wanted to send a resume of my undergraduate achievements to the colleges that denied me acceptance, just to prove that their admissions standards were somewhat flawed, but regretfully I never did.

After a semester at Columbia Law School, I enlisted in the Army Reserves and spent 1958 in basic training at Fort Dix and then was stationed at Fort Knox in Louisville Kentucky, in their parts supply school, graduating at the top of my class, which would come back to haunt me later when I was recalled to active duty to fill that slot for an activated upstate reserve engineering company.

I returned home in March of 1959 and married my high school girlfriend in mid April, living in a one bedroom apartment in Freeport. I went back to working for my dad's firm, Vogue Jewelry, where I had spent some time laboring in the summers while attending school. I had started as a messenger and worked my way thru almost every segment of the manufacturing process, ending up in the shipping department where I learned about production schedules and distribution to upscale retail outlets, both large and small.

I continued to work for Vogue instead of returning to law school as I now needed to earn a living. Coincidence would have it that the head of the shipping department left the company shortly after I had started working and I was promoted to the manager of that department, and was raised from $ 75 a week to $ 150 as I was now a married man and had to support a wife that was finishing her college education at Hofstra University.

I eventually "found my calling," when I was promoted to showroom sales. Knowing my product so well, I evolved into a successful salesman as I came across as both knowledgeable and sincere. In later years, at Les Bernard, I insisted on my sales staff understanding the entire process of designing, manufacturing and marketing of our fashion jewelry, and because of their knowledge, they too were all considered sales professionals.

I was working full time and attending Army Reserve meetings every Monday night and spending two weeks each summer with my battalion at an Army camp either at Fort Drum in upstate NY or at Ft. Lee, in Leesburg Virginia. As a result of my college education and typing skills, I was given the opportunity to work in the office of the supervisor of the 42 St. armory in NYC. He was not a member of the military, but rather a civilian employee of the Department of Defense. I and two other privates would do all the necessary typing, which included disjointed bits and pieces of the "gangster" novel he was in the midst of writing.

My wife gave birth to our first child, Lauren, on January 6th, 1961 and at this point I wished to stop attending the weekly meetings, and that leads me to bring you to the event of me being assigned to a control group (one that had no weekly meeting obligation, but still had a summer camp commitment). My experience of being assigned to a control group is the subject of a rather lengthy narrative that is detailed in the addendum section.

In 1961 Toby & I had already purchased a home in Lakeville Estates in East Hills, when I was recalled to active duty for the Berlin crisis. I invoked the Soldiers and Sailors Relief Act which protected recalled or drafted servicemen who had signed any kind of contract as it placed that contract "on hold" until the serviceman was released from active duty. So although we were the first "tack on the board," we were the last couple to move into the development, and the builder used our home as his sales office during my tour of duty. I can still remember the look of astonishment on his face when I told him of my situation and that he had to "hold" the house for me. After checking with his attorney, he sheepishly agreed that I was correct and that indeed he would honor my contract when I was discharged.

We finally did move into 74 Tara Drive in 1962 with our eighteen month old daughter and our new born son. We were living the "standard life" of a newly married young Jewish couple in East Hills, socializing with most of our neighbors on a regular basis. In late 1966 strange things started to happen that led me to suspect that my wife was being unfaithful and I confronted her. Naturally, she denied it, but I just could not get those well placed suspicions out of my mind.

Then in 1967, when Marc's accident occurred, I knew that I could do nothing until I made every effort to rehabilitate him or finally accept the fact that he needed to be placed in a facility. Sadly, even during Marc's patterning, my wife managed to pursue her relationship which by then I had fully documented. I knew that it was just a question of time when I would be free to separate and divorce, as I could not endure the pain of her betrayal particularly in the midst of grieving for my son, and I desperately wanted to be out of the marriage.

In retrospect, I am sure the strain of our situation with Marc contributed to the breakdown of our marriage, but being unfaithful was something I could neither comprehend nor accept. I flew down to Tijuana, Mexico and obtained a divorce decree and shortly thereafter, Toby and the girls moved to Forest Hills.

Let me now refer to the years following Marc's accident, as I was still in the early stages of growing Les Bernard and it was not easy to focus on both aspects of my life as I was also trying desperately to maintain a good relationship with my two daughters that were living in Puerto Rico.

After the two year stint in San Juan, Toby returned to Long Island with the girls and her attorney husband and settled in Rockville Centre, which was certainly more convenient than Puerto Rico for visitation purposes.

By this time, Laura and I were married and living in Muttontown and my daughters visited on a regular basis. In the summers we picked them up on Thursday evenings and traveled out to Shelter Island where my twenty four foot Chris Craft Lancer was docked at the Deering Harbor Inn. We spent just about every summer weekend out there, and our relationship with the girls was getting back on track.

17

Events then started to take place that led us to believe that Toby's second marriage was starting to unravel as she was "seeing" an antique dealer on the sly who had a store in Rockville Centre, aptly named " The Artful Dodger." It seemed that Toby's mother was working in the store and she introduced Toby to him and they commenced an affair that eventually ended up scuttling her second marriage. Obviously, this was her modus operandi, and so it was that she imminently moved with the girls into her mothers' house in Rockville Centre with her new boy friend, a Mr. David Herley.

Toby told us that David was a very wealthy divorced man who owned a brass foundry and was in the final stages of negotiating the sale of the business to a Japanese company for eleven million dollars, and they were looking at a million dollar town house in NYC, and had hired a very prestigious town house architect to draw up renovation plans.

We became suspicious when Mr. Herley started to carry on over every dollar that was being expended on behalf of the girls, claiming that I was spending more on my three Great Danes than on my children and "he was not going to stand for that."

Concurrently, at this time, Toby started filling my daughters' heads with strange stories about Laura and me that led to the girls not wanting to come and visit. They were told that we were taping them when they visited the house, and we were meddling in David's personal affairs, and trying to interfere with their relationship, none of which was true.

Once again I found myself hiring a private investigator as our suspicions were running high about Mr. Herley's character and integrity, and we shortly leaned some very shocking news that precipitated yet another major turmoil in my life, and the life of my two daughters.

Firstly, we leaned that Mr. Herley was still married to his first wife, Josephine, who was living on welfare with their two daughters in an attic apartment in Bellerose, Queens.

Secondly, we learned that the "Artful Dodger" antique store was now shuttered and in arrears for NY. State sales tax deficiencies, and that numerous judgments had been issued against Mr. Herley.

Further, his NY. driving license had been suspended for multiple infractions, and that he had no interest in any brass foundry, and in fact was employed as a detail man for one of the cigarette companies, and was being sued by that company for illegal activity. What a shock to learn that Toby's new beau who was then living with her and my two daughters in her mother's house, was nothing but a con man.

We made an appointment to sit with Toby and reveal all of this to her as we were truly concerned for her and the well being of my children. She refused to believe any of our comments and was in total denial. She went on to inform us that the foundry sale was imminent, and in fact she was taking the girls out of the Rockville Centre school system and enrolling them in the Lincoln School in New York City, in anticipation of their upcoming move into their newly renovated town house.

She refused to accept any thing we had to say; even when we revealed that we had visited with David's wife and children and learned of his fantasies. We told her that we actually sat with Josephine in her in her attic apartment and met his two daughters, and was informed of David's delusional mindset.

At this point, I again hired a divorce specialist, and after reviewing the situation, he agreed that it was indeed timely and appropriate that I try again to gain custody of the children, who were now living with an unemployed man of questionable character, and being subjected to his lies and fantasies.

Toby hired a hot shot Brooklyn divorce attorney and the case was soon on the calendar in Nassau County Family Court. The trial was swift and although the judge concluded that Toby was living with, and subjecting the children to a man of questionable character who was not gainfully employed, and living off the proceeds of the sale of our marital home and Toby's mother, and subjecting the children to an unhealthy atmosphere, it was not enough for him to wrest custody from their birth mother.

In addition to once again being denied custody, Toby told the children that I was trying to "steal them away" from her. It was indeed frustrating to me that I could offer the children a much healthier family atmosphere, but was once again denied that opportunity, and my repeated attempts to gain custody were always used to turn the children against me. As a result, Lauren stopped talking to me and stopped visiting, although Elissa did still come sporadically by herself.

A few weeks later, Toby enrolled the girls in the Lincoln School and proceeded to drive them in to Manhattan every day and pick them up after school. This move astounded me, as I knew there was no money to pay for the school, and I did not understand how Toby and David could spend the better part of every day driving to and from NYC with the girls.

Two weeks into the school year, I called the comptroller of the school and introduced myself. I informed her that although I was a very concerned father, I was in no way responsible for the girl's tuition, as they had ample access to a public school in Rockville Centre where they were currently residing. She then looked up their records and was shocked to see their listed home address on Long Island, and she also noted that the normally required school deposit had not yet been paid.

I explained that it was doubtful that the tuition would be paid and requested that she call me when the school had run out of patience with Toby and David. I received that call just before Thanksgiving when the school informed me that the children had "been removed from their respective class rooms for non payment of their tuition."

At that time I was told by the school administration that Mr. Herley could not pay the tuition, as he had to undergo emergency heart surgery in Houston, Texas with Dr. De Bakey. I replied that I doubted the validity of that, but I well understood their position in the matter.

When I contacted Toby to let her know that I was aware the children had been ejected for non-tuition payment, she was shocked that I was so informed as she had no idea I was monitoring the situation. When I asked her where the children were currently enrolled in school she was evasive and refused to give me any information.

The month of December pretty much was over when Toby's distraught mother called and pleaded with me to institute yet another custody action as the children were just hanging out with Toby and David in her house and she was concerned for their welfare. My attorney immediately contacted Toby and told her if the children were not enrolled in school by the first week in January, that he would indeed be instituting yet another custody suit on my behalf.

A week later, we were informed that Lauren was enrolled in a high school in lower Manhattan and Elissa in a public school on East 33rd St. as that was around the corner from the luxury apartment building on 34th st. where Toby and David had just rented a three bedroom apartment(what happened to that million dollar town house??).

Of course I wondered how they were going to pay the rent on this apartment when David had to undergo emergency heart surgery with De Bakey in Houston, which of course I knew was an untruth. I called the comptroller of the landlord and related my tale of woe to a sympathetic lady who was also a mother of two young children. I explained that I was not calling to start any trouble, but merely to ask that if and when they found it necessary to order an eviction notice, they would give me "a heads up" so I could "rescue" my two daughters.

It was just a matter of months after they moved in, that I got the call, but not nearly in time, as shortly thereafter that afternoon, Lauren, my 16 year old, appeared at my showroom with a suitcase and asked if she could come live with us as the marshals were evicting them from the apartment. I asked why she didn't bring her nine-year-old sister with her and she replied that her mother would not let her.

Lauren did move in with us and was promptly enrolled at Locust Valley High School for her Junior and Senior years. Upon graduation, she attended Drake University in Des Moines Iowa and came home for holidays and for the summers. In late May of 1982, Lauren, unfortunately was involved in the most notorious crime spree incident in Nassau County when she was a hostess at the Seacrest Diner on Glen Cove Road and that story is detailed in my postscripts.

When we flew out to Des Moines for her graduation we met her boy friend who we quickly determined was really not an appropriate person for her to be with, but much to our chagrin, she decided to stay out there with him living in what was more or less a green house. Six months later, she came home for a weekend to talk to us, but it was really to borrow $ 10,000 so she and her friend could start a hydroponic tomato farm in their residential green house. After some discussion, I politely declined and asked her to please come home, but she was extremely miffed and left the next day, and that was the last time she "lived with us" or communicated in any way for some time.

I kept track of her and learned that she and her friend had moved to St. Thomas in the Virgin Islands where they were employed on a hydroponic farm, but that did not last very long and the next thing I knew they were living with her grandmother who had since moved to Ft. Lauderdale.

A short time later I was informed that she had secured a job as a manager of a storage facility which included an on site apartment that she was sharing with her Des Moines friend. That situation lasted a few months and the next thing we knew he and his dog took off for the mid west and Lauren was now living alone and managing the storage facility which was located in Davie, a suburb of Ft. Lauderdale.

We had purchased an apartment in Palm Beach and Lauren did come up to visit once or twice, but only after I had driven down and tried to re establish some sort of relationship with her. In late 1986, she informed us she had met one of the storage facility's clients, who was in the air conditioning business, and they were dating

21

and she wanted me to know he was Jewish as she probably thought that would please me. My reaction was more of shock than acceptance as this was the first Jewish boy she had ever dated.

Approximately six months later Lauren told us that she and Larry were engaged and wished to plan a Florida wedding. At this point she had "wised" up to her mother's new husband David (who I learned, had never divorced Josephine, and technically was a bigamist) and asked if Laura and I would make her a wedding as she knew her mother could not afford to do that. My father was fiercely against that as Lauren had not spoken to me for some time nor had she communicated with him or my mom prior to her passing. I thought long and hard about that, but decided to err on the side of "doing the right thing" as I knew my ex wife and her "husband" could not afford to make a wedding and frankly, I could. With Marc's accident, the divorce and ensuing years of strife, the road had been bumpy enough for all of us and I felt obliged to give Lauren a fresh new start to what I hoped would be a happier life. Additionally, it was my mothers dying wish to me and Laura "to take care of Lauren."

Lauren, Laura and I planned the affair which was held in the Governors Club in West Palm Beach overlooking the Inter coastal waterway and Palm Beach Island. We had one hundred guests to the June afternoon wedding, which was lovely, and we avoided any incidences among the four sets of parents attending (Larry's parents were also divorced and both remarried), as we strategically sat each couple and their guests at the other three corners of the room. As she was departing, my ex "threw me" a thank you and that was our first communication in years and the last to this day.

During the intervening years, Lissie would visit with us on a very limited basis as she was receiving some very poor information from her mother blaming us for all the trials and tribulations that they were encountering and no matter what we said, we were "the bad guys." However, in 1984 she did manage to accept our gesture of throwing her a rather spectacular sweet sixteen hill top pool party with a chartered bus delivering all of her Forest Hills friends to our home.

In the early 90's after having sold our Florida apartment, we returned to St. Martin for our vacations and we ended up renting either a three bedroom apartment or a villa and everyone was invited, so that meant we were there with the four girls; Brie with Todd, Blair with her date at the time, & Lauren with Larry and Elissa. All seemed hunky dory and I was delighted that all my girls were again communicating.

Shortly thereafter, we learned that Toby and her "husband" had moved with Elissa to an apartment on East 10th st. in NYC where I believe she and David still reside.

As anticipated, we never did hear anything further about the town house or the foundry.

Elissa, who had recently returned from the University of Arizona, was seeking employment and I introduced her to a poker friend of mine who was in the party dress business, and she favorably impressed him in her interview and started working in his showroom.

Shortly thereafter, Laura and I had lunch with Elissa and she confessed to us that David had molested her when she was younger. I was livid, but both Laura and Elissa convinced me not to confront him nor report him to the authorities. I reluctantly agreed, but insisted on her moving out immediately.

We located an apartment for her on the upper West Side and moved her in within a matter of days, and I paid the rent and supplemented her salary for the three years she lived there. Again, I had tried to "do the right thing" in spite of the treatment I had received from her in years gone by. After all I was her father and I did give Lauren a wedding so I felt compelled to "rescue" her from living in an unhealthy atmosphere once again.

She did well in the job and started to travel internationally for the company; presenting it's collection at trade shows in England and Germany and she relocated to the Upper East Side.

She eventually left that company and accepted a position with Dana Buchman as their sales representative at Saks 5th Ave. where again she seemed to do quite well.

She called us one day and said she was seeing a gentleman and wanted to bring him out to meet us as they were getting engaged!!! Honestly, I was a little taken aback as I had never heard anything about this "guy," but Laura, Blair, and Brie knew she was seeing a man of color but had never told me. I was not really upset, but just concerned for her happiness and well being.

She visited us with the gentleman who was quite nice, though a bit older, with a twenty four year old daughter of his own. Laura prepared a lovely lunch which she served in the dining room, and we had what I thought was a very pleasant and meaningful conversation. I pointed out that I hoped they would think a little about it and suggested that perhaps he should move in with her (he was living in Chicago at the time) and give it a six month trial, as they certainly would experience some adversity with an interracial union and we just wanted to make sure they were both prepared to deal with the anticipated problems. I also mentioned that I had heard from her uncle Lenny (my ex brother in law who I remain friendly with to this day) that they had already planned a July wedding in a NYC townhouse but they both denied that, and I accepted what they said at face value.

Laura and I felt the conversation went well as there was no confrontational attitude on either side, however I never heard from Elissa until mid May, fully seven weeks after the lunch. When she did call I explained that I was a little upset in not hearing from her after the luncheon, but she countered "well you could have called me." I patiently explained that after we had gone out of our way to be more than accepting and hospitable, it would have been appropriate for her to call us and just say thanks.

Obviously she disagreed as two months later, in July, we learned that they were indeed married in a town House in NYC. So in fact she had lied at lunch that day.

I was not invited to the wedding, nor have I ever heard from her since, and to add salt to the wound, I was told that David "gave her away." Through the grape vine we learned that she was divorced within a year and she is now re married to another gentleman of color and lives in New Jersey and has two children, but to this day I have never heard from her, even when I know thru friends, that she was aware of Laura's passing.

As to Lauren, we did have a relationship and interacted with her whenever we went to Florida, or when she came up North to visit or to attend the U.S. Tennis Open as she was an avid player and fan. During one of the visits in the early 90's when she came up with Larry, she asked if it was alright to visit Marc, as she had not seen him in all the intervening years. Of course I said it was fine, and I arranged for her to visit that very day.

She returned early that evening and said she was surprised to see him sitting up in a wheel chair, as she had envisioned him all those years as being bed ridden and hooked up to a life support system, and she wanted to know why he was not living with us. I attempted to explain how emotionally difficult it was for me over the years and how stressful it was to visit, and that after making sure he was well cared for, there was little else I could do.

I carefully explained how bringing him home to live would have seriously impacted the entire family twenty four hours a day, and I did not feel it would be beneficial enough to Marc's well being to inflict that burden on everyone else. In addition, "I preferred to remember Marc as he was not as he is." She was not happy with my response and returned to Florida obviously upset.

Two months later she called and invited ME to visit them, ostensibly to observe the progress they were making on the building of their home on the five acre site they had purchased in Davie. She made a point of not inviting Laura as she also wanted to talk to me "daughter to father."

Both Blair and Laura (Brie was away at Bucknell) cautioned me not to go as they were sure she wanted to discuss "the Marc situation." In spite of their admonitions, after my son in law called and said I should come down and speak to Lauren alone as she had something important to discuss, I did in fact fly down solo.

What greeted me at their home was a replica of Marc's "sailor" room in Roslyn prior to his accident, but now with wheel chair access, and a plea from Lauren and Larry to let them take Marc out of the Long Island facility to live with them full time.

The conversation eventually erupted into a major disagreement when I attempted to explain to them that I could not in good conscience allow that. I ended up flying home the next morning, as they both said some pretty nasty things to me. A few days later I received a letter from Lauren telling me what an embarrassment I was to her as a father as she felt I had abandoned Marc all those years and it was cruel of me not to let him come and live with her. She concluded by saying that she no longer wished to communicate with me.

I responded with a lengthy letter of explanation to let her know why, although I respected her desire to care for Marc personally, I could not let him be removed from the Malvern facility. I tried to explain what pressure that would put on her marriage, emotionally, physically and financially as Marc's needs were perpetual, requiring full time care and in the event of serious illness or necessary physical therapy, the costs would be enormous and not sustainable by either her or me. (I had previously received an invoice from the cerebral palsy center he attended in the amount of $ 400,000 for services rendered during the preceding year). My words of explanation fell on deaf ears, and eventually she lobbied the Malvern staff to arrange for a hearing to determine Marc's living arrangements.

Naturally, I was invited to attend the hearing as was his mother along with Lauren and Larry. I, as his father and legal advocate since he was 18, was asked to speak first, and after I presented my feelings in a very logical and parental manner, they asked Toby for her opinion and she said and I quote, "I agree with everything that Bernie just said." So having both the biological mother and father concur, the case was closed and Marc was to remain in the Malvern facility. However, as a peace making gesture, I did agree to allow Lauren to take Marc for a two week visit each year during the Xmas holidays as long as I was notified in advance and gave written permission.

To Lauren's credit she did that for about four years until Marc got violently ill on one of the visits and Lauren, realizing she could not deal with the situation, returned him post haste to Malvern, and to this day has no longer requested that he visit with her. I think, hopefully, that maybe she finally realized the situation was significantly beyond her ability to cope with, and that his needs were best served by remaining in a clean, professionally staffed, full care facility, with a nurse and doctor on call.

Lauren has never spoken to me since, even when she learned of Laura's passing, so obviously, Marc's accident in 1967 has seriously impacted my life these last forty-six years, and will continue to "haunt" me.

I pray that I outlive him so I can insure his well being for the duration of his life span. I do visit when my heart dictates, and of course I remain totally involved in all decisions that affect his daily life.

He is never out of my mind or heart, ever!!!!!!!

I am thankful he is in a wonderful facility within ½ hour of my home which has enabled me to "sleep in peace" and rebuild my life over all these years.

For the record, on those occasions when all four of my girls were interacting either at our home, or on vacation in Florida, Shelter Island or St. Martin, were among the happiest days for me, as it gave me an opportunity to have "my family" together once more. Sadly for all concerned, those circumstances did not last.

Those who knew me during these years realize that I managed to survive all of this by "soldering on," nurturing my second marriage, the development and success of Les Bernard, the estrangement of my two eldest daughters, the raising of Blair and Brie, the start up and growth of Muffin Lady, the Enron debacle, the running of a small local landscape company, working for the Village of Muttontown and since 2006, actual retirement.

Additionally, during all of this, we sold our apartments in both NYC and Palm Beach Florida. We again returned to St. Martin where we had vacationed with the children before we had purchased Florida in the mid 1970"s. We ended up selling our Palm Beach apartment in 1989 and NYC in 1995 after I had completed "my tour of duty" for the new Les Bernard.

Our first trip back to St. Martin was to La Samanna where we had first stayed back in the early 70's, but after a couple of visits to that great resort, we started to book villas on the French side as that offered us much more bang for the buck, and the kids and Laura, loved being in a house. We ended up returning on multiple visits with friends or family and ultimately in 1995, purchased a six acre water front site on Simpsons Bay.

We eventually split the property in half, sold off the lower three acre parcel, and in 2000 built our dream house on a bluff overlooking the entire bay, with the airport, downtown Marigot and the St. Martin Mountains as a lovely back drop. The view was "drop dead," and within two years that part of Simpsons Bay became the hot spot on the "lagoon" especially if you wanted your own protected boat facility.

We enjoyed our ten years in the house which was a rental property, as the income helped offset the high maintenance costs for an Island home. Once the Euro became the currency of record, things became a bit tighter financially, as all our income was in U.S. dollars and all the bills in Euros. The dollar was in a downward spiral and we ended up for the first time with a short fall relative to expenses.

It was then that we decided to sell St. Martin where the cost of living was rising daily, and purchase a mountain top parcel with panoramic mountain and ocean views on the Pacific West Coast of more affordable Costa Rica.

We finally closed on our St. Martin home in January of 2010, and it was shortly thereafter that Laura passed on. Although I still own the property in Costa Rica, I have no plans at all to develop it.

I have now entered the last phase of my life, satisfied that with the help of Laura for those forty years, I have always strived to "do the right thing—every time.

I have endured a lot over the last fifty-year journey, but in spite of all the trials and tribulations, I can still look back and feel that I have had a wonderful and rewarding adventure, and I recognize that that the total of my life experiences have made me the individual I am today.

That truly is an outline of my story and I am sticking to it!!!!

ADDENDUMS

On the following pages, I have attempted to relate some of the circumstances I referred to in the initial narrative, but now in somewhat greater detail.

Some are also "new" stories that I felt "stood on their own." I relate these vignettes as best as I can recollect, and hopefully, they will offer some additional insight into the multiple "soap opera" situations I found myself in over the years.

I have strived to keep them in some semblance of chronological order when appropriate.

Some are serious, some are humorous, but all contributed to making me the person I am today… a "sick puppy" who is still wagging his tail.

I am simply trying to "go with the flow," while dealing with the everyday matters of living that we all have to encounter; our health, financial responsibilities, family relationships, social obligations, or just the simple task of putting one foot in front of the other every waking hour of every day we have left on this planet.

I have chronicled these stories primarily for the benefit of my children, grandchildren and close friends, (some of who I hope may be interested) in the expectation that it enables them to have a greater insight into………

Who I was………… who I am ……….. and why!!!!

THE BAR MITZVAH BOY 1949

Birthdays were never a big deal during my childhood years. I am sure they were celebrated, but somewhat under the radar. Although that tradition continued through my adult life, I do vividly remember four of them that were celebrated, and I allude to them chronologically throughout this compilation, starting with my Bar Mitzvah.

I was raised in what I refer to as an untraditional Jewish home with a very strong, wise, unconventional father, and a very sweet, charming. nurturing mother. As you may recall, I originally "roomed" and communicated with my maternal grandfather strictly in Yiddish until I was five, when we moved out to the suburbs and he went off to remarry. OMG, I now realize how difficult it was for my mother and her two sisters to accept his new wife, which if my memory serves me correctly, they never did!!! And that is a situation that I now have a much clearer insight into.

Birthdays were really low key, and truthfully I do not remember any until I was approaching my 13th, and strictly because of my grandfather, I was placed on the path to having a Bar Mitzvah.

I was enrolled in Hebrew School which I resented, as it interfered with my play time after school, but I "took it like a trooper." About two months into the semester, I was expelled for biting my teacher's finger. When asked for an explanation, I declared, "he was always picking on me and shoving his finger in my face and this time when it came to rest on my nose I just opened my mouth and bit down." In my circle of friends, I was the only one ever expelled from Hebrew School, and it was a badge of honor and distinction that I wore with a great deal of pride.

So now how was I to prepare for my upcoming Bar Mitzvah if not enrolled in Hebrew School? Aha!!!! My dad went to speak to the Rabbi who informed him he could hire the Cantor who would get me up to speed, and that would be acceptable. After his discussion about the date of the great event with the Rabbi, my dad negated a traditional Saturday morning Bar Mitzvah, as the Rabbi indicated it would cost $ 100 for the temple and my dad bristled at that sum.

The Rabbi said if money was an issue, I could have a "no fee" Bar Mitzvah on a Thursday morning by joining the early morning congregation and saying just two short Berakhahs and laying Tefillin. My dad immediately embraced the concept, especially knowing that my tutoring would now be minimal and relatively painless for me, and of course, less costly for him.

And so it was that I found myself one Thursday morning in late March of 1949 along with my parents, my two aunts & uncles and grandfather at the Rego Park Jewish Center at 7 AM to "celebrate" my 13th birthday. I distinctly remember that my grandfather was not accompanied by his second wife as either she was not invited or had since passed. I know not which, as we really had lost all communication over the preceding eight years while he was living up on the farm, but I suspect she was not invited.

By 8 AM all of us were back in my parent's apartment for bagels and lox, and I then received my three fountain pens and well wishes.

Promptly at 8:45, my dad said "ok Bernard, go get your books and I will drive you to school." My relatives were aghast that I was being ushered to attend class on this, the very morning of my Bar Mitzvah, but out we went, and for the first and only time, I was driven to school. By 9 AM I had received congratulations from all my friends who were jealous that I had evaded six months of Hebrew School and had to say only two short prayers "to become a man."

My parents elected not to have a traditional Bar Mitzvah party which they viewed as a celebration for the adults and very much not a party for the children, so a gala affair at the temple or local catering hall was never "on the table." Who knew from fancy venues and country clubs back then?

Now lest you think I was deprived of a festival, hold on!!!

That very Saturday, my parents took me and fifteen friends via subway, into NYC to the New Yorker Hotel, where we had a ring side table for the ice show. The dance floor in front of us miraculously "disappeared," and then appeared an ice rink and a small very talented troupe to perform within "touching distance."

After the show, we were ushered back to Rego Park, again by subway, (no chartered buses or limos) to a carnival that was taking place right on 63rd Drive and Queens Blvd.

The sixteen of us were then let loose to enjoy the Ferris wheel, the Whip, the Swings, the Caterpillar, and all the arcade games and cotton candy we could inhale. For two uninterrupted hours, we all had a ball and for months afterwards, every one of my friends said it was the best Bar Mitzvah party ever, as it was just for us kids.

How times have changed, as now the carnival is brought inside to the kids, but it is not quite the same.

Kudos to my parents for focusing my Bar Mitzvah celebration on just me and my friends.

Just for the record, two weeks later, they hosted an adult celebration for their friends at home.......... I was not invited!!!

I now realize why I "march to a different drummer" as they say. My parents raised me with a markedly different set of values and principles than most of my contemporaries and that has forever guided me through life and influenced my decisions, and for that I remain extremely thankful.

I know now that their early teachings enabled me to "think for myself" all these years and to take actions that I deemed appropriate even when my choices flew in the face of conventional wisdom.

How ironic it was that some twenty two years later, at age thirty five, that I married a lady who was even more untraditional and unconventional than I, and that together we would take some very unorthodox initiatives.

ATHLETICS 1949-1950

I entered Halsey Jr. High in the fall of 1949 as an 8th grader full of athletic ambitions. I loved playing sports as I was a fairly decent athlete for my age and size (short and chubby), and my 8th grade basketball team made it to the finals against older and much taller 9th graders and we were clearly the underdogs.

Our team was lead by my friend Elliot who was a decent ball handler and our prolific leading scorer. At the end of the fourth five minute overtime the Principal, Dr. Nussey, was ready to call it a draw, but Elliot and I successfully pleaded for just one more overtime session. Obviously our opponents doubled and tripled teamed Elliot as they thought for sure he was the "go to guy" for this last period, which is why I found myself with the ball pretty much unguarded and about twelve feet out on the side of the paint. In spite of Elliot's continuous "calling for the ball," I took a bank shot that went cleanly in and put us up by two points with a minute to go. We were successful in holding the 9th graders scoreless on their possession, and again I found myself in pretty much the same location, with Elliot screaming for the ball, and again I banked in a clean basket and we were up by four with thirty seconds to go. As they scored, time ran out and our 8th grade underdog team toppled the 9th grade by a score of twenty to eighteen, and that, after regulation and five overtimes. Hey, a win is a win and we were the school basketball champs.

The following fall, my class fielded a pretty darn good softball team and I either played second base or right field. We went undefeated for the six game season and we all received miniature metal softballs, which I hung on a chain and sentimentally eventually gave to my daughter, Elissa, when many years later she attended Halsey.

It was shortly thereafter during my first year in High School that I joined a softball team called the Crescents as most of the players lived in that area of Rego Park. We were definitely "not the team to beat" as there was another neighborhood team called the Wings, which I tried out for but did not make. They were mostly older, bigger and stronger, and we were always considered the "minor league team" compared to their "major league status."

They thought of us as the losers, and they pretty much refused to even play us, lest their sterling reputation be besmirched for beating a group of "bush leaguers." I finally convinced my friend Larry, who played third base for the Wings that they needed to engage us as we all thought they were overrated. I guess I goaded him into convincing his teammates that they had to shut us up once and for all. I think what prompted them to comply was when I told Larry we would just show up at their field every Saturday morning, earlier then they would, and occupy the field which was at PS. 139, my elementary school. So if they wanted to avoid that, they would have to play a scheduled game with us at their home field.

The game was set and the Friday night before it was to be played, Larry called me and said they would have to cancel the game as the umpire they used was sick and could not make it. My dad, overhearing this, volunteered to umpire the game. I told him "dad, they are not going to agree to that if I am on the opposition team." Larry overhearing this said "hey we all know your dad and if he wants to ump that would be great, because I know he will be tougher on you guys than on us." And so the game took place.

Now let me digress for a moment to give you some background here as it is important if you are to understand and appreciate the "whole story."

My dad was himself a darn good softball pitcher and first baseman and he played pick up softball every Sunday morning at the same PS. 139 field which was large enough for the older guys. You see, we on the Crescents were used to playing on a much smaller field at a school located in the middle of the Crescent neighborhood. PS. 139 was like a major league park to us with the left and right field fences being a good three hundred feet and center field (normally the longest of all) was just two hundred and fifty feet due to the vegetable garden that was tended by the elementary school students. Any Saturday or Sunday game at this site drew a crowd of fifty or so spectators as the competition was first rate, and they knew they would always be treated to a competitive game, no matter who was playing.

The Saturday prior to the game, we practiced at PS. 139, just to get familiar with the "park" as most of my teammates had never played there. During batting practice, which I was pitching, I noticed my father had showed up to watch us.

When it was my turn to take batting practice, I asked him to please leave as I did not want him to observe me hitting as well as I did, as I did not want to disappoint him at game time the following week. He left, but unknown to me, he turned the corner of the school and hid under a doorway and observed me drilling the ball over the left and center field fences, so he knew I was a powerful hitter which I am sure made him feel better about agreeing to umpire the game.

We won the coin toss and elected to be "the home team" and the Wings jumped off to a two run lead on their first at bat and you could see the smirks on all their faces, as if their original thoughts of superiority were already borne out.

34

I batted in my regular # three spot, as although I was a fairly good hitter, I was not considered powerful enough to be in the "clean up spot."

My power was always to right or right center as I took a "two step" into the pitch, and consequently my bat was always a little "out front" resulting in usually a line drive to the right side, but not over any fences.

On my first at bat, I was called out on strikes by my dad on three pitches that were clearly balls. I knew then that if I wanted to contribute with my bat, I had to swing at anything that I could reach as my dad would be inclined to bend over backwards to "call against me," in his effort "to be fair."

In the third inning I came up with men on second and third with two out and after my dad called two strikes on high pitches, I stepped out of the batters box and said, " hey at least call them close." I blasted the next pitch over the center field fence, which was a ground rule double, and the game was tied.

In the fifth inning, their power hitter, Ira, drilled a hit to right center which I raced over to cut off and as he decided to stretch the hit into a double I wheeled and threw a line drive strike to second which arrived when he was still three feet from the base. He turned to stare at me in amazement as none of them had any idea as to just how competitive we were.

When I batted again, the Wings were ahead by a run and again I had two men on base in scoring position, and not taking any chances with "the blind ump," I swung at the first pitch and blasted it over the center field fence once more, scoring another two runs and putting us ahead four to three. When I reached second and looked back at home plate, I could see just the slightest smile of pride on my father's face, but of course he continued to call a very tight game and indeed was quite fair.

We eventually won the game seven to four and the Wings were in shock by our performance. To his credit, Larry came over and congratulated us saying they had no idea we were so competitive and they wanted a re match.

He asked me, "how come you never told me you were such a good hitter ?" I replied "you never asked, and you never even let me hit during my try outs for your team."

The next game was played at Crescent Field and we triumphed once more. We never heard from the Wings again, and we then learned they had disbanded shortly after our two drubbings of them.

After another year, we too all disbanded after three very successful and rewarding seasons as we were all now caught up in our high school activities.

I now know the lesson I learned here was that you should never be intimidated by other's apparent abilities, but rather just focus on your own, and do the very best you can with what you have. We played as a cohesive team and we overcame their superior strength. They were cocky and we were determined and persistent, and that overshadowed whatever physical superiority they in fact possessed.

Who knew then that I was experiencing a valuable life lesson while playing softball with friends?

THE SWIMMER 1952/1953

I graduated Halsey Jr. High in June of 1950 and entered Forest Hills High School in September of that year, looking forward to participating in some extra curricular activity, namely swimming.

Alas, the teachers who coached extra curricular sports went out on strike for both my sophomore and junior years and it was not until my senior year that I had the opportunity of joining the swimming team.

Let me set the stage for you by saying I had never swam competitively, but rather just recreationally either in camp, on vacation in Florida, or during the summer months in the ocean first in Far Rockaway then in Atlantic Beach and later at Long Beach. I thought I was a pretty good swimmer so I was sure I would "make the team."

Since Forest Hills High had no pool, our tryouts were held at Jamaica High about a thirty minute train ride and walk from my apartment. I vividly remember sitting in the stands as the other free style swimmers tried out and then it was my turn and although I thought I did well, I was not among the finalists. Then came the breast stroke try outs and I watched forlornly as I knew I was not making the team. Lastly came the call for back stroke swimmers and amazingly no one raised their hand, so I did, and it turned out I was the **only** one that tried out for the team in that stroke. So guess what? I made the team in a stroke I had never really specialized or practiced, but since I was the only one to try out, "**I was it**."

Practice started the following week and we all had to travel to Jamaica where we were allotted one hour for practice, twice weekly. Now if you know anything about competitive swimming, you need to be in the pool at least two to four hours **every** day, so to say we were under practiced would be a gross understatement.

I along with a couple of my friends did manage to swim on Saturdays at the Shelton Hotel pool in NYC where Buster Crabbe was the aquatic director, but it was certainly not a supervised intensive workout. So yes we did get in a few hours there, but not nearly enough if we were to be competitive. It was what is was, and I was delighted just to be on the team.

Our first meet was against Bayside High School, the reigning City champs, and as luck would have it the PSAL champion back stroke swimmer was still there in his senior year.

The hundred yard event began, and by the end of the first lap I was two body lengths in the lead and my ecstatic team mates were poolside cheering me on. By the second lap I was one body length in the lead, and by the third lap I was behind, and in the fourth and final lap I could just about raise my hands out of the water. My teammates, no longer ecstatic, had to literally haul me out of the pool lest I become the first swim team member to ever drown while competing.

The Bayside home team bleachers, filled with about a hundred onlookers, went from shock, after the first twenty five yards, to hilarious laughter, as the match ended and I was unceremoniously lifted out of the water.

It was certainly at this point in my life that I learned what the term "pacing your-self" meant. I just did not have the stamina to maintain my original speed and I could not finish the race nor get out of the pool with out the aid of my team mates. (Some of whom were doubled up with laughter too).

I persevered and swam the rest of the ten meet season as the sole back stroke swim-mer for FHHS, but thankfully I had learned to slow down and at least finish the rest of the races without being helped out of the pool.

Each team fielded two swimmers in each event, but as I was the only back stroke participant for my school, I finished third in every meet, save one. It was the morn-ing after the last meet of the season, when I was having breakfast with my dad before he left for work and me for school. He was reading the sports pages of what was then the L.I. Daily Press and he turned to me and said "Bernard, I see you finished sec-ond yesterday, and I am really proud that you stayed with it and improved to take second at the last meet of the season."

I looked him squarely in the eyes and said, "Thanks dad, but just for the record, Jamaica had fielded only one swimmer too." We both laughed and in retrospect, it was during this conversation that I realized, you may not always be the best, but you always need to do the best you can.

I did the very best I could, and I earned my Varsity letter and jacket and wore them proudly for the last few months of school. I have both my certificate and letter framed and hung in my Long Beach apartment. Also included in the frame is a pic-ture of me at sixteen, proving I did (and still do) have six pack abs, but they are now camouflaged by a few inches of added skin.

If and when the conversation arises about me being a competitive swimmer, I always tell people, "yes in 1952/53, I was the # 1 backstroke swimmer at Forest Hills High," and by god that is the truth.

A year of so ago, my friend Ardith inquired about my broad shoulders and I replied, "It's because I swam back stroke competitively in high school." She responded, "Oh I knew it had to be something like that," and now if she reads this book, she knows the unvarnished truth about my aquatic career.

To this day, I am a stronger than average swimmer, but like the golf and tennis pros in their respective venues, the really competitive swimmers "float" in a very different pool.

This experience taught me not only how 'to pace myself thru life" but the rewards of persistence as well, and perhaps most importantly how to be self deprecating and laugh at myself without being embarrassed, which is a quality that has stood me well over the years, as I often found myself in less than optimal situations that required a good sense of humor in order to survive.

CLARK UNIVERSITY...FIRST EXAM SCARE 1953

All male freshmen at Clark were brought on to campus in late August, a few days before the semester began. We were then all bussed up to a camp in New Hampshire ostensibly for three days of aptitude tests, but mostly to bond by sharing our high school stories, playing ball, and dining together.

It was during this orientation that a few of the other guys hanging out at the basketball courts started to bug me about trying out for the J.V. team as they noticed my very skillful passing ability. All "shooters" are anxious to team up with good playmakers, as they crave the ball and love to be on the receiving end of some very sharp passes, especially when it leads to easy lay ups.

I told them I was not sure about that as my first priority would be my academics, but secretly I was dying to play on the team and was intending to attend the tryouts in mid September. That was my plan until my very first exam in General History 14, a course emblazoned in my mind forever as you will soon understand.

GE 14 was a basic core history course required of all liberal arts students so many of my dorm mates were also in the class. The professor told us we were having a quiz the following Thursday on the first three chapters of the assigned book, and I remember studying those chapters until I had all the facts and dates down pat. I walked into the class room and there on the board were two essay questions asking for an analysis of two situations in the book, and I freaked out. I never really had essay questions in high school, but rather either true or false or multiple choices, and now I had to analyze what I had reviewed, and my mind kind of went blank. I left the room knowing that I had flunked my very first college test. The following Tuesday my worst fears were realized as I received my test paper back with a big F in red with no other comments. Just a big fat F. I returned to my dorm room in a cold sweat feeling that I had let myself, and more importantly my parents, down after just two weeks into the school year, and I panicked about flunking out and the reverberations that would have at home.

I immediately knew that participating in any sport or other extra curricular activity was out of the question, as my academics were priority # one. Consequently, I never did try out for the JV basketball team which was a great disappointment. Instead, for the next four months I buried myself into my studies and in my next GE 14 test I earned a C, than a B and then on the mid term an A and again an A on the final.

Dr. Jordan wrote on that test that in all his years of teaching he had never had a student go from an F to an A, and he commended me for my dedication and perseverance. I ended up fourth in my class that first semester and thereafter my grades were no longer a problem, but sadly, the first year went by without any real participation in anything extra outside of my studies.

I did make the JV in my sophomore year and in today's terminology was the starting point guard. I made the team primarily as a passer and play maker as my scoring ability was minimal and probably good for only six to eight points a game, but my assists were always in the double digits so I was an important cog in the wheel. I thoroughly enjoyed my season of competitive basketball as we did travel through out the New England area, playing schools in our category such as Bates, Bowdoin, Assumption, Coast Guard Academy, and other small liberal arts schools where athletics were certainly not the prime focus. We had a losing season, but it was a hell of an experience for me, but in spite of encouragement from the coach, I did not try out for the varsity as by then I was too immersed in the weekly school newspaper as the Business Manager and besides carrying quite an academic load I was also very much involved in Phi Alpha fraternity matters.

My only other athletic participation during college (we did not have a swimming team) was as the student manager of the baseball team. Now manager back then was an administrative job. I was more or less the secretary that took care of team logistics, correspondence and finances and was also the official scorer at every game, so in fact I did earn two letters at school, one for the JV basketball and one for varsity baseball.

My folks were on vacation in Marathon, Florida when in the spring of 1957 I received official notice that I was elected as a member of Phi Beta Kappa.

I vividly remember my parent's elation at the long distance news. After profusely congratulating me, my dad who never got past 8th grade, sheepishly whispered, "by the way, what is Phi Beta Kappa?"

AFTER CLARK

My good friend Paul Shapiro and I were pretty much on the same path in college, excelling in academics, and participating in numerous extra curricular activities. Paul was president of our fraternity, co editor in chief of the year book, and a member of Gryphon the senior men's honor society, and graduated with departmental honors in Business Administration; whereas my academic accomplishments were in the School of Liberal Arts.

Our parallel achievements, not to mention our identical last names, prompted our parents to offer us both the same graduation gift; our choice of a six week trip to either Europe or a motor trip through the States. Paul and I opted for domestic travel and we took off in mid June in my brand new 1957 Olds convertible for an adventure that covered 12,000 miles over six weeks and every baseball or football venue in some thirty states. It turned out that we both made a good decision, as the two of us enjoyed extensive international travel in our later years, both for business and pleasure.

We pretty much got along for the entire trip except for one night in Las Vegas. Up until now what happened in Vegas has stayed in Vegas, but some fifty six years later it is time to come forward with the story.

After checking into a nearby motel, we visited the Sands Hotel, and lost a few dollars at black jack, but then noticed that Frank Sinatra was appearing that night and we went over to the maitre'd who informed us that we would have to wait in line, but if we came early he would assure us of a table up front. I slipped him $10 (hey it was 1957) and assured him we would return early enough to be near the head of the line. We returned to the motel, showered and I thought we were getting prepared to return, but Paul said he needed a nap and would I mind going over first and reserve our spot.

By 9:15 the maitre'd informed me he could no longer hold our table if my friend was not there. I stormed over to the motel and woke Paul up and carried on unmercifully as I could not fathom that he would allow us to blow a front row table at a Sinatra performance. We did not really talk for two days and to this day he has never offered me the $ 5 which was his share of the up front money to the maitre' d. Officially, I am still pissed at him for that incident, but now some fifty six years later, he continues to laugh it off.

In September of 1957 he attended Columbia University's MBA program on a two year full scholarship from the Edward John Noble Foundation (The owner of Life Savers), as he had been selected one of the outstanding national college graduates of that year.

I attended Columbia Law School with a full scholarship…from my parents.

Paul determined after our road trip that he would never again live on the East Coast and true to his word, after he received his MBA he has resided either in Southern California, Portland, Oregon, or for the last 20 or so years at the Boulders in Scottsdale, Arizona.

Of course he has managed to come here every summer for those last 20 + years, if for nothing else, but to escape the summer heat in the Phoenix area.

He has remained a bachelor with numerous long term relationships, while I have been married twice with five children, but we have always enjoyed and maintained our friendship notwithstanding our geographical distance and respective marital circumstances.

I am proud to say that we have now been close friends for 60 years!!!!

MY ILLUSTRIOUS MILITARY CAREER 1958-1962

After taking a leave of absence from Columbia Law (yes technically I am still on leave as I did have passable grades for that first semester), I enrolled in the Army Reserves and was promptly shipped to Fort Dix for basic training. I must note here, that one of my college roommates preceded me at Ft. Dix, so he filled me in on all the things I should expect which turned out to be quite helpful.

After our first long march, we returned to the barracks, exhausted, sweaty and very hungry. Everyone else discarded their gear, washed their hands and ran up to the commissary for diner. I remained behind and took a real good hot shower and went to the PX for a hamburger. When I returned, all I heard was everyone bitching about the lack of hot water, and I sheepishly got into bed and went to sleep.

In week three I was given the 12-2AM coal watch, which meant that one of the other trainees would awaken me at midnight, when his watch ended, so I could stoke the coal fire and make sure we had heat before I awoke the next person on watch. I did bank the fire, but then closed my eyes and fell asleep so I never woke the "next in line" and obviously neither did he. Thank god the fire lasted, as I did find out later, "sleeping on watch" was a court marshal offense, but no one else gave me up as they would have had to implicate themselves as well.

On the morning of "day and night training" I reported in as sick (as advised by my college roommate) as I was told it was the worst day since it required crawling under barbed wire while the machine guns (with blanks of course) were firing overhead. I and my friend went on "sick call," and we realized just how lucky we were when all the guys returned later that afternoon with bloodied knees and elbows and torn clothes. Knowledge is always power and I was lucky to have received a "heads up."

When basic training was over, everyone shipped out but I never received an assignment, so I remained in the barracks, helping out in the captain's headquarters awaiting my marching orders.

When the next set of recruits arrived, I and my buddy Jerry, another "holdover," were assigned to barracks # 2 as Leroy Washington, the regular platoon sergeant, was on a three day pass and we had to "shape up" the new arrivals on those first few days. Now Jerry and I were the only two Jewish guys in the company and we knew "all eyes were on us," so when the recruits arrived late that first afternoon, we gathered them on the second floor of the barracks and started to drill them in "fall in, attention, at rest, right and left and about face, forward march, etc, etc." The next morning when all four units had to "fall in," our platoon stood tall and followed every command as if they had been doing it for a week or so———as opposed to the other three platoons that were totally discombobulated.

After breakfast, the first sergeant came over to Jerry and myself and wanted to know how we managed to "shape up" those bone heads overnight, and we explained that we kept them up until eleven, until they got it right. He shrugged his head and shoulders and walked away.

Jerry and I were shipped out the next day. I guess our recruit training skills were not really welcomed nor appreciated.

He was shipped to Ft. Hood in Texas, and I was dispatched to parts supply school at Ft. Knox in Louisville for an eight week training course even though I had just ten weeks left to serve. It made no sense to me, but hey this was the Army Mr. Jones so away I went.

I was discharged at the end of March of 1959, just in time for my wedding which was scheduled for April 11th. Toby and I honeymooned in Jamaica and returned to a one-bedroom apartment in Freeport L.I. and she returned to Hofstra to finish her college requirements. I went back to working at Vogue and in August I was promoted to the head of shipping and received an increase of salary to $150 per week which was the exact amount of our monthly apartment rent, as that was the accepted ratio back in the late 50's.

After two years of living in Freeport, we put a down payment on a house in East Hills, Roslyn, and shortly thereafter our lives were thrown into turmoil as I was recalled to active duty and assigned as the parts supply clerk for the 969th Engineering Company from Tonawanda NY and off I shipped to Ft. Bragg for what turned out to be a ten month tour of duty.

THE GODFATHER POSTER STORY - 1959, 1972, 2010

In August of 1958 I joined the 214th Quartermaster Reserves (a bread baking unit) at the 42nd St. Armory in New York City and was promptly sent to basic training at Ft. Dix in New Jersey, and then on to Ft. Knox where you now know I attended parts supply school, achieving the then highest test score recorded in the schools history. This prompted the commandant of the school to request that I "re up" and he would them immediately promote me to sergeant and put me on his teaching staff. When I informed him I was getting married in two weeks back in NYC, he said to bring my wife down and he would arrange really nice housing and a cushiony teaching position for me. Obviously, I declined his generous offer.

Upon my discharge in April of 1959 I was married and lived in Freeport Long Island, but working in New York City and started to attend Monday night weekly reserve meetings.

After two weeks I managed to get "a job" as a clerk typist in the office of the Dept of Defense employee Director of the Armory. I was one of three young men typing in the office. The other two were Long Island boys too; Marty xxxxxx from Great Neck and Gerald xxxxx from Long Beach

The director was a squat cigar chomping gruff man who dressed in a tee shirt and short sleeve vest a la Art Carney of the Jackie Gleason show.

Besides any official Army documents, we did a substantial amount of typing for his personal project as he was an aspiring writer. We all typed a few pages of his work as he assigned it, and of course he carefully collected the work as we left for the evening. None of us ever got to see what the other person was typing, nor were we given anything with any continuity to type, but rather disjointed pages or paragraphs.

He was quite influential in the set up there so when I wanted to get into a control group (precluding attendance of the weekly meetings) he was the man to see.

He informed me it would "cost me" to get into a control group and that if I wanted to proceed I should meet him at a certain bar in NYC with "the consideration" wrapped inside of a folded newspaper.

Two weeks later, I received official notice that I had been placed in a control group. My attendance at weekly meetings was no longer necessary, but I still had to attend a two week summer camp with my unit which I did in 1960 at Ft. Lee Virginia, and in 1961 at Ft. Drum in up state NY.

In 1961, I received a notice that I had been reactivated and was assigned to the 969th Engineering Company of Tonawanda NY and was to report to Ft. Bragg, in Fayetteville, North Carolina to join the unit as their parts supply clerk. What a shock to my system, as I already had my first child and my wife was newly pregnant with my second child and I had a business in NY.

I of course went back to "my director friend" to see what had to be done and he told me he could not help me as this was the real deal. JFK had called up the reserves for the Berlin crisis, and if I wished I could go down to 1st Army headquarters in New Jersey to plead a hardship, which of course I did, but to no avail.

Shortly thereafter I was at Ft. Bragg where I joined the engineering company and remained for ten months and became the battalion ping pong champ. So much for my earlier outstanding test results at the parts supply school in Ft. Knox

While on duty at Ft. Bragg, articles appeared in the NY. Times and Herald Tribune calling attention to a scandal at the 42nd St. Armory where a certain civilian employee of the Defense Department was found to have been involved in wrongful acts. Some of the reservists that were implicated, and the individual (Mr. Goldman), were being prosecuted by the Federal Government.

However, the article did not mention the gentleman that I had "done business with" who was of Italian descent, and no one from the government ever contacted me.

In May of 1962 I was honorably discharged and informed that my military obligations were now considered fulfilled as I had served my country on two separate occasions. Just for the record, my baking company was never activated, so I ended up hurting myself with my "control group" coup. Purposefully, I never returned to the 42nd st. armory after being discharged.

Now let us fast forward to 1972 when I am married to my second wife, Laura, who was a Navy nurse herself, serving during the Vietnam War at St. Albans Naval hospital. We lived in the city and one night decided to go see the new hot movie *THE GODFATHER*. We entered the theatre and the credits started to roll and said it was based on a novel by Mario Puzo. I leaned over to Laura and said how unusual a name that was, and that I once worked for a fellow by that name doing some typing for him at the 42nd st. Armory back in 1959. As the movie developed I was almost jumping out of my skin as many of the scenes were familiar to me as I know I had typed something very similar thirteen years earlier. Could it possibly be the same Mario Puzo? No!, no way. !!!!! Then about a week later either on the news or a TV program they showed a picture of Mario Puzo accepting some type of film award & I said *HOLY SHIT* that is the man I worked for and "did business with" back in 1959.

Basically, I had no proof of any of this until twenty two years later when in 1994 while walking down the street in Great Barrington Mass. I spotted Marty xxxxx walking down the street towards me. He looked at me and we immediately embraced and he said, "Bernie can you believe that we typed part of *THE GOD-FATHER* novel and up until this moment I do not have anyone to vouch for that, but now we have each other." I said "Marty I can not believe we did that and thank god my wife can now at least have the account verified by you." Holy Toledo, what a story. I never saw Marty again, but at least Laura and the friends we were with had my yarn verified by one of the other typists.

So that is the reason I have an original numbered poster of *THE GODFATHER* mounted on my wall. I obtained it from my friend Glen who has a storage facility and discovered the poster in 2010 among the items he had confiscated due to a non-payment. When he told me that he had the poster I said "it belongs to me," as *THE GODFATHER* anecdote is one of the most bizarre and amusing sagas in my life.

THE BIRTH & DEMISE OF LES BERNARD INC.
1963-1996

When I returned home from my ten month tour of duty at Ft. Bragg, Toby and I moved into our new home in East Hills and I went back to work at Vogue Jewelry. By this time my dad's partner's son, Donald, had joined the firm and theoretically we were the heirs apparent to the company which was a well established leader in the fashion jewelry business.

Unfortunately, my dad and his partner started to have some disagreements about the roles their respective sons were to play in the business. I had already "graduated" from the shipping department into showroom sales and my father's partner wanted his son to do the same. In retrospect, my dad was right, as Donald in his short sleeve shirts and cigars, was just not "showroom material," and his work ethic at the company was not on a par with mine. So me, Mr. Goodie two- shoes, was at the apex of the problem and the better I did, the more the dichotomy was exacerbated until it reached major proportions and my dad and his partner agreed to "a divorce" with my dad being bought out and retiring. The harder I had worked and the more I learned and accomplished, the poorer I made Donald look. Trust me!! That was never my intention. He was a nice young man, but his heart was "into cars," and that is where I am told he ended up years later.

To his credit (and I guess mine), my dad's partner, offered me a position with the firm at an elevated salary, but I told him it would be impossible for me to remain after the nasty way he and my dad had split.

So, I was now unemployed and everyone was expecting me to return to law school, but let us remember, I now had two children, a newly purchased home, and a mortgage to pay, so it was a "no brainer" for me to get a job.

My phone started to ring with calls from other well known jewelry manufacturers asking me to meet with them for the purpose of "bringing me on board." After a few interviews of this nature, I turned to my dad and said "what should I do?" His comment was, "son, if all these companies are seeking you out there must be some word on the street that you are a potential asset, and if they all think you are such a valuable commodity, I suggest you consider going in to business for yourself."

I was astounded that he was willing to "bank roll me" and even suggested who I should go into business with, as I did need an "inside man" to oversee our detailed production and supervise the factory.

While at Vogue, we had employed as an outside contractor an "old world" Hungarian model maker/stone setter and his wife, who reliably manufactured a very high quality product and always had come thru for us. Lester Joy was then 59 and his wife a year younger, and I doubted if they wanted to go into business with a young man of twenty seven who they hardly knew. I was shocked that they jumped at the suggestion of starting a new company with me and my dad "in the background."

Within a matter of weeks, Les Bernard Inc. was born, with both Lester and I investing $ 25,000. Of course my capital was in the form of a paternal loan which I am proud to say I repaid in full a few years later with accumulated interest. We quickly rented showroom space at 417 5th Ave, and a five thousand sq. ft. factory space at 20 West 37th St, which was a literally around the corner from the showroom.

Now I must interject at this point that my dad had been approached by another young man who was seeking his backing to also start a fashion jewelry business. After numerous conversations, Mr. Harold explained to him that he "had to go with his son," and so it was that Kenneth J. Lane started his own company at just about the same time as Les Bernard, but without my dad's involvement. Of course anyone familiar with the industry would know that KJL became the most well known of jewelers and was probably the single biggest factor in creating a market for high fashion jewelry back then and for the ensuing years. Thanks to QVC his company still exists. (Sorry dad. you win some and you lose some!!!!) We went head to head with KJL from 1964-1991. He certainly had more industry, consumer, and fashion magazine recognition, as he was "socially connected," but Les Bernard faired mighty well in those years and my dad never regretted his decision either intellectually, emotionally nor financially.

We spent the better part of six months creating our initial collection which we knew had to be a "knock out" if we were to gain instant notoriety as my dad's reputation was kind of on the line and everyone would be curious to see how "the sought after son" did after the father had left Vogue.

In all honesty, at the inception of Les Bernard, although I had a "good eye," I was not really very accomplished in the design end of things, but my dad certainly was. He had been the creative force at Vogue for over twenty five years and he was determined that our first collection had to be a blockbuster that would get the industry talking about "the new kid on the block." My dad, known in the industry as Mr. Harold, was a true innovator, and I readily admit that without his experience, creativity, and guidance, Les Bernard would never have happened.

In our first collection, he designed moveable flower pins (for which we received a U.S patent), created a "new faux pearl" that he named twilight to reflect the hue of the essence, and introduced genuine marcasite on gold plated metal (when historically it had always been set into rhodium plated metal) which gave the jewelry a totally new and warmer appearance.

With these innovative looks and genuine Wedgewood beads, Les Bernard introduced itself to the market in June of 1964.

Bergdorf Goodman was the first to advertise both the movable flower pin and the twilight pearls. Those two ads in August and September, instantaneously propelled Les Bernard into the forefront of the fashion jewelry industry, where I am proud to say, it remained for the remainder of its existence.

For the first six months, I worked seven days a week, presenting the collection in our 5th Ave. showroom during the day, taking home the orders booked that day and compiling production tickets that evening at home, which I then delivered to my partner in the factory the very next morning. I then went in over the weekend to be the "shipping clerk" for what we had produced that week.

Finally, we were able to start hiring staff: first a shipping clerk, then a bookkeeper and then an assistant designer to help my dad with the creative end of things. Yvette came to us from Hattie Carnegie, and immediately bonded with us and when my father retired, she served as the head of the creative department until I sold the company in 1991.

We then hired Ms. Glory the manager of the Vogue Jewelry showroom, who after seeing the new products we were unleashing, called us and said she wanted to leave Vogue and come to Les Bernard to work for Mr. Harold and Mr. Bernard.

Glory was our sales directress until her retirement in 1990, and I must say she was unquestionably the most respected saleswoman in the industry. Everyone knew and loved Glory and she loved Les Bernard. Glory and Yvette both enjoyed twenty five year anniversary celebrations with the company. Yvette opted for a full length mink coat and Glory for a gala party at the Water's Edge restaurant with thirty five well known industry guests.

My dad remained active for about 10 years until 1973 when he and my mom moved to Palm Beach so he could enjoy his golden years, which he did until his passing in 1987. Lester and Sunny remained until 1974 and they too wanted to retire to Florida. I then purchased Lester's share and at the age of thirty seven, I became the sole owner and chief cook and bottle washer at what was then a $2,000,000 company. By then we had moved our factory to East 19 St just off of Park Ave as we needed more space and we signed a ten year lease for seventy five hundred sq. ft. which we quickly absorbed. It was now circa 1975 and Laura and I had started our international traveling, and from that point on I took total charge of our development and growth. Under my dad's tutelage I had honed my sense of style and color and with my romancing of the semi precious gem business, Les Bernard entered another round of significant expansion.

When Lester retired, I hired a family friend, Dick Hane, to manage the factory and he too became a fixture in the company until his untimely demise in the late 80's. During his management years, knowing that my "back was covered" from a production and shipping viewpoint, I was free to concentrate on design, and sales, both domestically and internationally.

We eventually had over 100 employees in our NYC production facility and six territorial road salesmen with six permanent showrooms in New York, Atlanta, Dallas, Los Angeles, Chicago, & Minneapolis.

In addition to periodically visiting each of those showrooms during their trade weeks, Laura and I were now traversing Europe and Southeast Asia, "discovering" unusual raw materials for development within our design department that now numbered five; Yvette, two associate designers, and two administrative assistants to handle all the follow up detail work required in fashion jewelry design and production.

It was in 1974 that we made that first trip to Asia, establishing a business relationship with Mainland China, and very gingerly "dipping our toes in the water" with genuine ivory, which I thought might be of interest to the American market.

In the years to follow, ivory became the single most important semi precious product that Les Bernard offered, and we ultimately became known as the "king of the fashion ivory business" with national ads running in Vogue, Elle and Harpers. We took ivory out of the "basic" it had been for so many years consisting of plain bangles and buttons and turned it into a fashion statement by creating stylish pieces, mixing the ivory with other semi precious stones. Our national ads were accompanied by local full page retail ads by Bonwit Teller, B. Altman, Neiman Marcus and many other well known retailers through out the country.

We enjoyed our ivory dominance for ten years, when finally the U.S. Fish and Wildlife service declared ivory to be on "the endangered species list," and the importation and selling of any ivory became illegal in the States. Consequentially, Hong Kong, the center of the ivory business became devoid of all the ivory carvers as they all had to switch to bone as a replacement and it just did not have the look or cache of genuine ivory. I must add that in all the years Les Bernard sold and promoted genuine ivory, we always had our shipments accompanied by a certificate of "legal kill," which meant our ivory came from only legally culled herds. (Or so the certificates stated).

I vividly remember Neiman Marcus calling me when the U.S. ivory ban was announced and asking me how much inventory I had on hand for immediate shipment. We had at the time approximately $ 50,000 in beads, plaques, bangles and buttons and they took EVERY piece, ran a full page ad in Dallas and sold it all out, and that was the end of the ivory era as we knew it. In 1990, trade in ivory products was banned internationally.

However, we still had our coral which now we were importing not only from Naples, but from the South Pacific as well and of course we did have a "one time" promotion of lavender purple coral, which no one had ever seen before, or since. We ran a full page ad in Vogue on a purple branch coral necklace and it was a complete sell out.

We were on a roll but exhausting the existence of "new" semi precious gems as we had already offered, ivory, coral, tiger eye, jade, lapis, sodalite, onyx, tourmaline, peridot, topaz, rose quartz, amber and mother of pearl so we were "running out of steam"— until to paraphrase, " a funny thing happened on the way to the TV."

I received a call one day from Helen Galland, the former President of Bonwit Teller, who now had her own fashion consulting business. She told me that Dynasty, the TV program was looking for a quality manufacturer to create, produce, and sell a Dynasty fashion jewelry collection and she had recommended Les Bernard based on her experience with us as a quality manufacturer and our reputation for "doing things the right way." I jumped at the opportunity and signed on for a two year licensing deal not knowing exactly what to expect. I was given a mandate to create a hundred piece Dynasty- like collection which would have to meet the approval of both Esther Shapiro, the shows creator, and Nolan Miller, the designer of the Dynasty clothing. Two months later I was on a plane to LA. with a hundred and five pieces of "Dynasty" type necklaces, pins, rings bracelets and earrings for a presentation to both of those people. They were astounded at what they saw, and promptly commissioned ninety eight of the creations, which became the first

"Dynasty for TV" collection by Les Bernard. The faux diamond jewelry was simultaneously presented in two hundred stores throughout the country and the PR we received in the press from Women's Wear, the NY Times, the NY Post, Soap Opera Digest, and all the local fashion columns around the country was unbelievable. We enjoyed a great spike in our volume, as many retailers who had not previously carried our collection then reached out to us. With Dynasty adding to our already established fashion business, our volume peaked in the mid 80's at just under $5,000,000, and we were no doubt "the largest" of the upscale domestic fashion jewelry manufacturers.

It was at this time that we moved our factory for the third time as we again needed more space and we leased a 10,000 sq ft facility across town at West 19St., in Chelsea (before it was chic). This was the ultimate jewelry factory, laid out quite efficiently and the largest fashion jewelry manufacturing facility in NYC. Here is where the initial Dynasty collection was shipped from in special Dynasty packaging and labeling, under my personal supervision. Yes, all those years later, I was back to being a shipping clerk, as I wanted everything to be perfect for the premier retail presentations.

After the two-year agreement expired, I decided to "back off" since I sensed the show was losing its popularity and as luck would have it, I was correct. The show only lasted another season or two, but Les Bernard had "moved on." Dynasty was not the only "designer line" we were responsible for as we also contracted to create collections for James Galanos, Mary McFadden, and Ugo Correani (an Italian designer of some note). All of these collections were successfully marketed and each one resulted in Les Bernard gaining additional notoriety and market share. We also had preliminary discussions in our showroom with Geoffrey Beene, Oscar de La Renta, and Aldo Cipullo (of Cartier love bracelet fame), but unfortunately those situations never materialized as all these talented gentlemen seemed more motivated by their projected royalties than in offering us any creative jewelry design input.

While all of this was transpiring, I had started to explore selling to Europe and Asia, a concept that no American fashion jewelry manufacturer had entertained up until that point. I along with one other costume jewelry company joined the Providence Jewelry Association in their second trip to the Basle Fair, where Les Bernard was very well received, and this opened my mind to attending other European trade fairs. And so began the Les Bernard saga of "doing Europe" for selling purposes. The 70's had been for buying and now in the 80's it was time for selling the Les Bernard look to Europe.(and eventually to Asia as well).

We first attended the Premier Class show in Paris at the Hippodrome D'Auetil which was a race track close to the 16th Arrondisment. The trade fair took place in the "infield" of the track. Imagine telling the taxi driver to drive us, with our two sample cases and advertising displays, into the middle of the race track when no one really knew about this set up. He could not believe it, but there it was, a very large tent set up in the middle of the infield as that is exactly where the show was held for the next few years. It was a heck of an experience to be showing jewelry and all of a sudden have everyone run outside to view the steeplechase as the horses galloped by. The show was very "high class" and it really turned us on to doing the European trade show itinerary for the next ten years right up until 1992, when we peaked at nine shows. We were now not only doing the Premier Class in Paris, but also the Bijhorca as well, and then the shows in Madrid, Milan and Frankfurt, in addition to private showings in London, Lisbon, Hamburg and Stuttgart.

Most trade fairs were held semi annually, but we could not possibly attend every show every time so we picked and chose which we thought would be most beneficial.

During our maiden trip to Madrid, on the last day of the show our booth was jammed all day and at 4 PM when the show was ending, we ran out of order books and had to borrow books from our French neighbor/exhibitor, (don't ask) and by 6 PM they were literally rolling up the carpets around us as our booth was still packed with customers. What an experience!! This of course brought us back to Madrid on three additional occasions, but for those visits we bought extra order books.

The Chibi in Milan was perhaps the most commercial and well attended of all the fairs, but quite frankly, it was more for the new Les Bernard in 1991 and 92, rather than the "old" Les Bernard as most of the attendees were wholesalers and distributors so they were looking for very reasonable prices for their rather large quantities as they in turn were selling to European retailers.

Paris was by far "our" market, as every fashionable retailer in Europe attended those two shows twice annually so we ended up spending quite a bit of time in gay Paris, not only when we were there for the fairs, but we did manage to spend weekends in Paris when doing business in other cities as we were never really more than an hour or so away by plane. We flew in each Friday night and caught a late flight back to our work city on Sunday night. Two days in Paris was "our vacation time," and we ended up in Paris at least two dozen times, either for business or pleasure or both.

How lucky could we be; Hamburg (or London, or Lisbon or Stuttgart etc) during the week and Paris for the weekend. That is why I have always maintained that traveling defined both my business and married life as Laura managed to accompany me on every trip (save one). It was a real bonding experience for us as the jewelry business was something a woman could get involved with, and of course she was a genuine asset when it came to socializing with our clients. It really worked well for some twenty-five years and represented a very large percentage of our quality time together.

Les Bernard's crowning achievement was receiving the coveted Dallas Fashion Award for accessories in 1988, which coincidently was bestowed on us as we were celebrating our 25th anniversary.

I accepted the award in front of two thousand retailers at the Dallas Mart and that evening we attended a black tie celebration at Neiman Marcus and were seated next to Johnny Versace and his bevy of European models, as he had been named that year's outstanding ready to wear designer. Naturally we had bought Brie and Blair with us for this award presentation, and the unexpected opportunity to "mingle with the Versace crowd" was quite exciting to them both.

As our distribution and volume increased, we outgrew even our 10,000 sq. ft NYC facility, so we reached out to a few quality Providence jewelry manufacturers who we started to contract out work to in order to alleviate the burden of producing everything in our own facility.

Yvette developed a close working relationship with a Mike Dipanni of Vanity Jewelry who was the only Providence manufacturer that was open to fashion direction and whose quality was up to Les Bernard's standards. Our business grew together, and soon everyone was commenting on the upscale fashion look of the normally commercial Vanity line, and of course we knew that Mike was "adopting" some of our input into his own line, with our approval, as it was a two way street. When we developed full confidence in his ability to manufacture and deliver to our quality standards, we actually turned over quite a bit of the Dynasty collection which was produced almost entirely in his twenty five thousand sq. ft. Providence factory. This was a mutually rewarding marriage and soon Mike was looked at as the fashion leader among Providence producers.

By 1989/90, the fashion jewelry business in the states was suffering greatly due to many upscale stores such as Bonwit Teller, B. Altman, Julius Garfinkel and the like going out of business. That coupled with the minimalist look in ready to wear was taking its toll on fashion accessory companies. To add fuel to the fire, many firms and retailers were now starting to turn to China for the manufacturing of product. Thankfully, while others were struggling to survive, our European and Asian business, allowed us to thrive.

Not withstanding the down turn in the fashion jewelry business, Mike yearned to own a 5th Ave firm with the cache he could never achieve in Providence, and so it was in 1991 that he purchased Les Bernard. He asked me to stay on in my role of CEO, but he wanted me to also become the international sales representative on a more permanent basis. We shook hands on a five year contract and from May of 1991 to mid 1996, Laura and I were on an international odyssey adding to what we had already experienced in the seventies and eighties.

Unfortunately, Mike did not quite know how to handle the domestic Les Bernard customers, most of whom were upscale dress boutiques who purchased small quantities of a style, as he wanted to sell in dozens and grosses. He closed our model 19th st. plant and downsized us into a much smaller facility on West 37th street as he had terminated most of my production staff, replacing them with of course his Providence crew. He basically used NY as his design and shipping point until he eventually decided to do all the shipping from Providence and he ended up closing us in NY. and moving the entire operation to Providence and eliminating almost all of our small upscale boutique customers. Simultaneously, we ended up closing our other area showrooms and terminating the road salesman as well.

He then downsized the New York showroom and eventually closed that facility also, and at the end, I showed the Les Bernard collection from our East Side apartment on 37th st. The few remaining customers came over to review the line there, but the hand writing was on the wall. Les Bernard as I knew it was to be no more. In the course of sizing down the number of accounts, he eventually managed to close out all of the customers that it had taken us twenty eight years to develop. He thought he knew how to run Les Bernard, but he just did not really comprehend what we were all about. When I left in 1996 Les Bernard was just about out of business and I was in "retirement" mode. A sad ending to a great success story, but Mike exemplified the true golden rule: "He who has the gold makes the rules."

Of course Laura and I were saddened by the turn of events, but the truth is that running an upscale fashion business such as Les Bernard for twenty eight years was extremely demanding and filled with the never ending pressure of creating hundreds of new styles four times a year; one collection for each of the seasons, with the added pressure of making sure those collections "were spot on and fashion forward."

Personally, I silently welcomed the respite. I had started the company when I was only twenty seven, nurtured its growth for twenty eight years, and enjoyed its international recognition as an industry leader, and ultimately its orderly demise. When I finally retired in 1996, I was sixty and it was time to take a long breath and relax.

I had enjoyed a lengthy run and all good things must come to an end, and I was certainly more than amply rewarded over the years for all the time and effort. In poker parlance, "you have to know when to "hold em" and know when to "fold em."

Now some twenty two years after selling Les Bernard, the fashion jewelry industry seems to be experiencing a long over due resurgence and I notice that some of the companies that existed back then, managed to "hang around" and are now "back in business," but I am sure almost all of their product line is manufactured in China as Providence is no longer the "costume jewelry capitol of the world."

Les Bernard creations are now considered by many to be "vintage" and fetch prices far exceeding the original wholesale or retail prices of the 60's, 70's and 80's.

I know that I made the right decision for myself and my family as there was no way I could have survived the extended fifteen year "drought" mentally, emotionally and financially. What was— was— and I am grateful to have had such an extended and rewarding career adventure.

The enduring personal satisfaction of seeing women wearing a Les Bernard creation, was, and still is, priceless.

THE DECORATORS, AMBIANCE AND IBIZA -1970's

When the lease on my NY apartment was coming due, Laura and I decided to purchase a two bedroom apartment on the Upper East Side of NY. I gave Laura a budget and told her to find a suitable residence facing the park on 5th Ave. After a few visits with brokers she told me that in our price range there was "no such animal," so we started moving East to Madison, Park, Lexington and finally on to 3rd Ave where we did in fact find a lovely three bedroom apartment that we liked, but it was 50% more than I wanted to spend.

So I said ok, let us look at waterfront property in Sands Point and I upped the budget a little. After a week of searching with brokers, Laura came back to report that my budget was still woefully below market price for what I was seeking. Hey $100,000 was a lot of money back in 1972 or so I thought.

My next step was to contact a Roslyn real estate broker on 25A, whose name escapes me, and I explained that I wanted a three bedroom ranch house with an open plan so that the living room/den would be adjacent to and open to the kitchen. (A little ahead of the curve back in 1972).

We met her the following day and she took us to Brookville and Pheasant Lane off of route #107 and showed us a house that exactly matched my specifications. I was astounded that overnight she had located a home that matched my requirements to a tee. Laura balked at buying the very first house we visited but she did agree that it was "built just like you specified," and it was on two acres and backing up to the Cedarbrook Golf Club. Two days later we had a deal and were ecstatic and we left for a Florida vacation with my two daughters meeting up with my folks in Marathon Florida.

Unfortunately, the seller "took the house off the market" a few days later so the deal fell through, but the truth was he received a bid for $ 10,000 more and sold the house to the new bidder. My broker was livid and sued him for her commission which she did in fact collect as she had "brought two parties together for a deal." She was happy, but we were distraught.

Months went by and nothing came up that appealed to us until one rainy Sunday morning, when we were spending the weekend in my parents Long Beach apartment, and we noticed an ad in the NY Times for a converted carriage house on three acres with rolling hills, lawn and woods.

The ad really appealed to us, and as it was listed by our broker, we called and asked why she had not mentioned this property. She replied "because it is almost twice what you wanted to spend." Laura said she would like to see it anyhow just for a reference point as we were not even sure what a carriage house was. Two hours later we were up on the North Shore about to enter the driveway at Ambiance when I bristled at viewing a home directly on a major highway. The broker though understanding said "well we are here and they prepared the house for a showing so let us at least show them the courtesy of looking." We were introduced to the owners Stuart Blaine and Robert Booth who it turned out were well known decorators on the North Shore with their own antique shop in Hempstead. After a cursory run thru we thanked them and left and Laura and I started to drive back to NYC on 25A when she asked me to stop at the Gulf station on Rt. 107 so she could make a call. I asked who she was calling and Laura replied, "your mother, to tell her we found a home." I said "are you crazy, it is much too expensive and I did not even look at it when we were there." She replied, "Bernie if I do not have that house I will die," and that is a direct quote.

We returned to the "scene of the crime" on numerous occasions during the next few months as Laura was truly enamored with the interior and to be truthful, I fell in love with the grounds. The decorators indicated that they had made numerous trips to Paris where most of the wood accoutrements in the house were from; including the living room Parquet de Versailles flooring which they were quick to point out was worth, at that time, $ 25,000. To that I quickly replied, "how about removing it and taking that amount off the price of the house." I immediately received a sharp elbow in the ribs and Laura blurted out "oh he is just kidding." I was not, but over the years I have come to understand the insensitivity of my naive remarks, especially to the two designers who lovingly had overseen the floor's installation, piece by piece.

So it was in April of 1973, after lengthy negotiations that we finally agreed on a price. We closed on Ambiance the following month with the decorators moving into the cottage, where they indicated they would be living for the two years it would take them to wind down their business. In retrospect that was not really true, but I believe rather a clever marketing ploy, which did in fact "lure us in."

Four months later they told us they had unexpectedly liquidated their entire inventory and were putting the cottage on the market and moving to Ibiza off the coast of Spain. We were under the gun financially, but did manage to come up with a down payment and they offered us a five year mortgage with a balloon payment, which then enabled us to exercise our right of first refusal.

There was no way we could allow the adjoining house to fall in to someone else's hands thereby eliminating our privacy and five acre "mini estate."

It turned out to be a good thing as the cottage has been solidly rented for the last forty years, with the first tenant staying twenty eight, and the current tenant being there over five. The rental income has more than covered any related cottage costs and property taxes, and additionally helped defer some of the landscaping expenses on the larger parcel.

We had established a really nice relationship with "the boys" as they greatly appreciated the fact that Laura was so in love with the house that they knew she would keep it looking "just right" over the years.

A few months later they contacted us and invited us to visit them in Ibiza which we knew nothing about as it was not yet "the international hot spot" it turned out to be in the 80's and 90's.

Since Alitalia was introducing a direct flight from Rome to Ibiza through Barcelona, we agreed to visit at the tail end of one of our numerous Italian coral purchasing adventures. It turned out that the maiden flight we had booked was delayed for twenty four hours, but we had no way of notifying Bob and Stuart as short of them picking us up at the airport we had no other contact information. Knowing my penchant for organizational details, I will never understand how I allowed that to happen, but it did.

We arrived the next day, but of course they were not there to greet us. Laura said "what the hell do we do now." I replied, "Leave it to me." We entered a cab and I asked the driver to take us to the best hotel in town, and he said there were two. So we stopped at the first one and I inquired if we had a reservation for the previous day, and they said "yes and we were disappointed in not seeing you." Laura was astonished and wondered how I knew where to go and I said, "Listen Bob and Stuart would not book us anywhere but the best place in town."

We were lucky it was the first of the two hotels we went to, however unluckily, they did not have any contact information for us. After explaining the situation, the manager suggested we visit the local police station in the morning as all foreigners residing in Ibiza had to register with them.

We arrived at the station house at 9AM the following morning but after an hour of searching their index cards (remember it was circa 1975), they could not locate our guys so the officer suggested we meander into town and take a seat outside of one of the busy cafes, and Bob and Stuart would "find us." Dumbfounded, I said "you mean they will think to stroll the avenue looking for us?" He replied "No senor, but everyone not working, roams the main street in the late morning, and I can just about guarantee they will appear."

Not having any viable alternative, we dutifully walked to town and relaxed at an outside table, sipping our espressos. Within thirty minutes, as predicted, along they came strolling, hand in hand. They were ecstatic upon stumbling on to us, as they had no idea we were even arriving after we failed to show as scheduled.

They quickly ushered us to their newly decorated home about 15 minutes out of town. Needless to say it was an impeccable converted "farm house" with all of their decorative flourishes just oozing out at us.

They had definitely "discovered" Ibiza before it became *Ibiza.*

Sadly, we learned they both passed away, Bob in the mid 80's and Stuart in the late 90's. Knowing the two of them was truly a delightful experience.

LAURA AT THE WHITNEY'S 1971-1990

As some of you may know, North Shore Hospital in Manhasset sits on land gifted from John Hay and Betsy Whitney, who maintained a close relationship with the hospital for many years.

When Laura was discharged from the Navy in 1966, she applied to the hospital as they had an opening for a supervisor on the pediatric floor. Laura in her inimitable style, having no pediatric nursing experience, still managed to secure the position as her resume included two years of Vietnam "war" experience at St. Albans Naval hospital. Naturally, in a matter of weeks, she was "running the show."

Her reputation as a caring, competent young nurse, made the rounds quickly. So when Betsy Whitney called the hospital to send over a nurse to care for her grand daughter, nicknamed Bebo, who had broken her leg and was now suffering from a case of chicken pox under the cast, the hospital sent over their youngest, cutest, most caring, charming, diplomatic nurse, Ms. Laura.

The Whitney family quickly embraced her presence in the house as she had a calming affect on the child and she quickly won the hearts of the entire household staff. It was here that Laura developed her taste of fine art as she found herself totally surrounded by it. One day she took Bebo out of her room to the grand living room to "change her environment" and she placed her on one of the couches. When Laura looked around she found herself staring at Monet, Renoir, Cézanne, Van Gogh et al. She knew they all had to be the "real deal."

She became familiar with the workings of the staff and especially friendly with the major domo, Emil, who really "ran the show." Here was Laura, a Bronx born girl of middle class Italian heritage, enveloped by the height of luxury, in a huge mansion on hundreds of acres, with a household staff, including chefs for just the help, chauffeurs, upstairs and downstairs maids, groundskeepers and butlers, all attending to only two inhabitants, Betsy and Jock Whitney.

The petite nurse from the Bronx, soaked it all in while caring tenderly for the grand daughter, which endeared her to not only the staff, but to the Whitney's as well, including Bebo's mom, Kate Whitney, with whom Laura maintained a close relationship for many years thereafter.

After Bebo recovered, Laura returned to the hospital where she soon was promoted to assistant nursing supervisor, however, not being comfortable with the politics of that position, she opted to became the head nurse in the newly formed radiology department.

In 1982 when Jock Whitney became ill, the call went out again and Laura now was sent over to care for "the man," which she did until his demise a few months later. Laura then left hospital nursing as she wanted to stay home and raise her children, but her "retirement" was short lived as Betsy Whitney became ill, requiring around the clock nursing care.

Although Laura did not "pull a lot of shifts," she organized a nursing team and supervised Mrs. Whitney's care for a few years until her Muffin Lady responsibilities required her full time attention.

On numerous occasions, I was treated to a visit to Greentree, viewing the art, the gardens, the indoor tennis court and even swimming in the indoor Olympic size pool. It was a situation that only a very few are afforded the pleasure of viewing, and even fewer the pleasure of experiencing on a daily basis. It was certainly a throw back to the 1920's/30's, and a way of life that hardly still exists.

Mr. Whitney was the US Ambassador to the Court of St James from 1957 to 1961 under the Eisenhower administration. Mrs. Whitney's dad was Dr. Harvey Cushing often called the father of neurosurgery as we know it today. This was truly a home of "blue bloods," but the Whitney's to their credit were "down to earth people," who truly cared for their help and that Laura could personally attest to.

All in all, Laura was professionally associated with the Whitney family for some fifteen very interesting years. During that time span, she met Joan Payson, Mr. Whitney's sister, and first owner of the NY. Mets, Bill Paley, Mrs. Whitney's brother in law; the head of CBS, and directors of all of the well known NYC cultural venues. It was a truly elegant experience.

BERNIE'S 40TH

At the end of March of 1976 Laura and I were ready to celebrate our 5th anniversary and my 40th birthday. Laura desperately wanted to entertain at home but wanted "something different." When Mrs. Whitney heard about this she suggested that she give some of her staff off one Saturday night and let them come over to the house and under Emil's supervision, create a "party to remember."

Well, it was not a very hard decision to make, and so it was that we had a very professional white glove staffed gala at the house.

We had over seventy five guests, which included both social friends and business associates (a combination we had never dared try before).

As there were too many for a sit down dinner, Emil suggested a very "high line" of hors d'oeuvre's which included filet mignon, shrimp, and unshelled lobster tails, along with all the "regular" hors d'oeuvre fixings which were served all night, so no one went home hungry.

We served only vintage champagne and wine, all selected by Emil and I am sure "borrowed" from the Whitney's wine cellar.

The evening was spectacular though understated, and quite special from beginning to end and those that were there, still refer to it as our "white glove" all night cocktail party.

Laura and I were always thankful for Mrs. Whitney's unsolicited generosity, but then again, Mrs. Whitney was eternally grateful to Laura for taking such tender care of her granddaughter and it was her way of saying "thank you."

It would take me another thirty years to have a meaningful birthday celebration (and our 35th anniversary to boot) which should give you some idea of how low key we played birthdays and anniversaries at the Shapiro household.

THE MUFFIN LADY SAGA 1977-1994

When my oldest daughter, Lauren, came to live with us she had put on a few extra pounds and fortuitously our friend, Carol Baim, had opened a "Diet Center" and Lauren started on one of their weight loss programs.

One of the essentials of the regimen was a home made sugar free diet bran muffin which Laura started to bake for Lauren on a daily basis. When she started to shed a few pounds she bought one of the muffins into the center so that Carol could sample it. The muffin was such a hit that Carol asked Laura to bake some for her center which she would sell to her clients.

At first Laura baked a dozen or so muffins for Carol which sold immediately, and then it was six dozen, and then twelve dozen, as other diet centers wanted the muffins for sale too. It soon became hundreds of dozens, as it was selling in about six North Shore Diet Center locations.

Shortly thereafter, Laura became aware of another lady baking similar products for the South Shore Diet Centers. They met and quickly formed a partnership, "The Muffin Lady," and they started baking in earnest in our kitchen and the two additional ovens Laura had installed in one of our staff bedrooms that was adjacent to our kitchen.

I was delivering muffins on the way to NYC to the stores en route. I would pull up in my chauffer driven Lincoln Town car, dressed in a suit and tie, and schlepping in anywhere from four to 12 dozen freshly baked dietetic apple bran muffins.

Laura was having apples delivered to our kitchen from a produce distributor and the entire house soon started to reek from a strong aroma of apples and bran. By 7 AM each day the kitchen was bustling with her three lady helpers and eventually her part time delivery man, as I had been mercifully relieved of that assignment. Three months later, I came in to the kitchen one morning and there were six ladies working and I said, "Laura I think it is time you moved out to a facility." She agreed and we then spent $ 10,000 converting the pump house in our court yard to a "mini on premises bakery."

Laura installed ovens and work tables, brought in a water supply, and upgraded the existing electricity that was up until then being used solely for the lights on the front entrance driveway gate.

After another six months of this, it was time to move on again, and Laura and Joyce rented a rather large space in Syosset and moved in all of their equipment. They were now in an official baking location which could handle the amount of supplies, (bran, apples, etc.) that they were now using on a daily basis. They purchased a wrapping machine, labeling machine, and apple coring devices, as they were now baking thousands of muffins daily.

This was now a real business requiring a full time commitment from both Joyce, who was driving up daily from her home in Valley Stream on the South Shore, and Laura who was now working from 7-7 every day.

What always amazed me was that during this period and into the future, no matter how demanding the business became, Laura always managed to make the international buying and selling trips with me, as Joyce would step up and bear the full burden of temporarily running the operation.

This was a very exciting time for the ladies as they continued to grow and hire administrative people as well as line workers. The operation started to produce substantial dollars every day enabling Laura to pay back her mom and dad who had loaned her $ 30,000 to finance the start up of the facility in Syosset. Laura hired a friend as a business consultant and he helped them grow and expand. They opened a retail store over the bakery and started to sell not only muffins, but soups and other healthy, dietetic foods as well.

News of the store and its success traveled quickly and soon came to the attention of Crain's and The Muffin Lady was featured in one of their articles about local businesses being started by women, as back in the 70's an 80's that was newsworthy fodder.

The success of the retail business encouraged all the old Diet Center owners to want to own a store and so it came to pass that the The Muffin Lady retail business was franchised and six branch stores opened in Great Neck, Ft. Lee, Forest Hills, two in Manhattan, and one in Rye

Rather quickly there were then seven stores in the tri state area and they were known as Diet Emporiums, as they were selling much more than just muffins, but other prepared foods and outsourced diet products as well. All the prepared food and muffins had to be purchased from The Muffin Lady, but the stores were free to purchase other approved diet products from out side vendors to add to their store mix. This added volume required Joyce and Laura to move to an even larger facility in Huntington, NY. where they established a Kosher USDA. kitchen. Now the ladies had over fifty employees, trucks, drivers, bakers, and cooks and an administrative staff of four. Certainly, this was no longer a "do it at home" pass time, but rather a substantial business.

The operation continued to expand until all the big wholesale bakeries entered the low fat diet muffin business, and the Diet Centers growth slowed and the stores also started to struggle and close one by one. Laura, never one to let the grass grow under her feet, became involved with the airlines through her chef friend Roy Daniels, and started producing first class meals for Air France, which turned out to be a life saver. She enjoyed a good year of that until some of the large airline caterers like Sky Chef became involved and she lost the Air France business, but ended up with TWA economy meals for all their international flights emanating from JFK. Muffin Lady food was on the ill fated flight # 800 to Paris which incidentally was the exact flight Laura and I took to Paris each time we traveled (timing is everything in life). They did receive a visit from the FBI after the flight blew up with their product onboard, but thankfully if was not the food that exploded!!!

The plant was churning out up to 10,000 meals daily which included some prison business as well. Finally, after a prison food riot, and the shooting down of flight # 800, not surprisingly, business started to dwindle. Her partner Joyce soon passed away and the burden of running the operation alone was starting to wear on Laura and she found a buyer to "take her out in whole." After almost twenty years in the food business, Laura, who temporarily consulted for the new company, finally retired and spent the next fourteen years performing private duty nursing for prominent families or chart review work for some of the leading medical insurance companies, which is how she was employed until April 28th, 2010, one day before her untimely demise.

LARRY THE GARDENER   1974- 1984

Laura and I were both known to "march to a different drummer" and the story of our landscaper and friend, Larry Zaino, was just such an example.

Larry had maintained my grounds in Roslyn for my 1/3 acre home site for most of the seven or so years I lived there. Naturally that relationship ended when I divorced Toby and sold the house.

In 1972 Laura and I took my two daughters on vacation to Disneyland and ran into Larry and his family, and I joked how I was going to permanently reside in the city so he would not have an opportunity to "get" me any more.

When we purchased Ambiance in 1973, I quickly called Larry and asked him to please help me purchase a sit down mower as I was going to do my own lawn. He chuckled, but obliged, and for the next year I did mow my own lawn, but it was a five hour task and when it rained, it ruined my entire weekend. To my further dismay, a few months later, my buddy George told me the grounds were starting to look a little seedy. So it was with hat in hand that I called Larry to please come over and give me an estimate for weekly maintenance, which of course he promptly did.

When we built the pool up on the hill, it was Larry and his crew that transplanted some of our large rhododendrons and pine trees that were located around the property to create a "privacy tree fence" in the pool area and, as in the past, he did a great job. During this period we became quite friendly and Laura invited Larry and his wife Gemma over for dinner which elicited a very negative reaction from some of our Roslyn friends who thought it undesirable for us to have a social relationship with the gardener who maintained our property. Paying no heed to our detractors, we did in fact establish a social relationship with the Zainos which lasted for quite a few years.

I relate this story, because soon thereafter Larry became ill and eventually moved back to Durazzano, Italy, a small village he had emigrated from years before. It seems his physician uncle was in charge of the diabetic clinic at the best hospital in Rome, and he went home primarily to be treated there and escape from some of the stress of doing business with his North Shore clients.

When Larry heard we were pursuing coral business in Torre del Greco and staying in Naples, he invited us to come and stay at his house during our very next trip, as he lived just outside of Naples. We politely declined as we were used to staying at the Excelsior, and were quite comfortable there, but he insisted and we relented. On the plane down from Paris, I consulted the Michelin guide to get some reading on Durazzano as perhaps that would prepare us for what to expect, but the village was not even listed. I turned to Laura on the plane and told her "we may be in trouble," but we were committed. Larry met us at the airport in a rather large late model Mercedes Benz and proceeded to whisk us off to his house that he said was forty minutes from the airport and up in the mountains. As we neared the mountain top we could see only one dwelling, and Larry confirmed it was his house.

We soon pulled up to a palazzo that was "out of a movie" with an automatic iron gate, ornate gardens and a true Italian fountain. We were then ushered to the detached two bedroom guest house, deposited our bags, and given a tour of the grounds that included a huge pool, tennis court, chicken coup and vegetable and fruit orchards all located on a thirty acre mountainside site with a panoramic view of the valley below. Well you could have knocked us over with an Italian fig, which by the way grew on the tree next to the pool. We ended up staying at his house on every subsequent coral buying trip over the next few years, and Brie ended up spending one summer there and in their Sardinian cottage, while baby sitting for his grandchildren.

On our "days off" we would either lounge by the pool, or visit local markets. It was seeing Italy thru the eyes of a local and nothing is better than that. We continued a very close relationship with the family for many years until Larry finally succumbed to the diabetes. He was the first friend that I had lost and he and his wife Gemma were among the sweetest people I had ever met. So much for not befriending those that work with their hands & come from humble beginnings. Some of those people are the salt of the earth!!!

THE "SHOOTING" OF MADONNA - AUGUST 1989

Laura and I wanted to expose Blair and Brie to the South of France, so we planned a vacation/business trip which ended up with us spending the last few days in Cannes, and then at the Hotel du Cap in Cap Antibes as we wanted the children to experience the ambiance of this hotel that we had previously visited with friends.

We had a jr. suite with the girls having their own "mini" room adjacent to ours. The very first day after lunch, we were up in the room when they started yelling and screaming and we rushed into their room to see them both "hanging" out the window staring at a lady walking through the garden patio. They blurted out, "that's Madonna." Laura and I had no idea who or what they were talking about. They grabbed Laura's camera, and shoved it into her hand and said, "take pictures." Laura put on her telephoto lens and started to snap away when all of a sudden, Madonna's rather large bodyguard, threw her to the ground and covered her body with his. Laura was appalled as she quickly realized the bodyguard mistook her camera and lens for a rifle and was protecting his charge. She quickly held up the camera so he could see it was not a weapon and only then did he get up wave to us and then help Madonna to her feet.

The girls then explained to us who Madonna was as they were so excited to see her and know she was staying at the hotel. A minute later we were visited by hotel security that checked us and the camera out. I thought, oh my god, we are going to hear from the management about this, but thankfully nothing was ever said. Two days later, we learned that Madonna was leaving and heading for Turin where she was "in concert." The girls made sure we positioned ourselves in front of the main exit and that their mother was "camera ready." As Madonna and her entourage exited, she recognized the girls and gave a friendly wave. Laura got some great shots and the next day, the hotel manager approached us and asked if after we had the film developed, he could have the negatives for the hotels' album. We happily complied. It was an exciting experience for the girls and of course Laura and I then became "Madonna savvy." I must add that we also "ran" into Johnny Carson and his wife in the garden, and Bill Cosby and his wife, in the lobby. Both were charming and friendly. Obviously, we were in the "right" hotel.

THE QUEST FOR GENUINE TORTOISE-1978

As most of my friends know, life with Laura was filled with many provocative, challenging, and funny stories all of which compete for "being the best," but since "the quest for tortoise jewelry" involved my business, and almost ended up with my incarceration, I guess it is the most poignant of them all.

We are in the late 1970's, and Les Bernard is now an established upscale fashion jewelry company, and Laura and I are traveling all over the world, seeking unusual gems to promote in the States, and one day my assistant tells me Gloria Fiore of Bonwit Teller is on the line. Now I must say, certainly I did receive calls from buyers from many of the leading retailers around the country, but Gloria Fiore was not one that made many of those type of calls as everyone was used to "calling her."

At that time, Bonwit Teller was already Les Bernard's largest customer (with Neiman Marcus running a close second) and Gloria had learned to both trust and like me, and she had really connected with Laura as well. She proceeded to say "Bernard, tortoise shell is going to be the fashion color for fall, and I have just come back from a three week European buying trip and I was not successful in locating any tortoise jewelry. I know you and Laura are about to embark on your spring buying trip, and I want you to locate genuine tortoise jewelry for me to promote this fall."

I am guessing it was around 1978, and Laura and I were indeed preparing for an extended motor trip through Italy, seeking coral, semi precious stones, silver and any other unusual raw materials that could be incorporated into our upscale fall collection, and now tortoise shell was added to our shopping list. When your most important customer gives you a marching order that is a direct buying assignment, it is not to be ignored.

Our Italian driver, Pietro Guerici was to be with us for the next few weeks, chauffeuring us around Italy, from Milan to Venice, to Florence, to Arezzo, to Rome and finally to Naples. In each city we visited, his assignment (after making dinner reservations), was to research the local yellow pages, seeking a manufacturer of tortoise jewelry, but they were non existent.

While that was his assignment, Laura and I shopped every better store in each city, but found only one "tortoise" bracelet, rimmed in 18 K gold and frightfully expensive.

So it was with a heavy heart that we finally arrived in Naples without a piece of tortoise to show for our efforts. We were relaxing in our room at the Excelsior hotel, another in the Ciga chain of fine hotels we were staying in throughout our three week voyage, when Pietro knocks on our door and excitedly says "hey there is one listing for a tortoise jewelry manufacturer here in town." That was the good news he said, but the bad news was the "factory" was located in a very "bad section" of Naples and he suggested that perhaps we should not venture there.

I said "are you crazy?" "We have spent almost three weeks seeking a source for tortoise jewelry, and now we have possibly found one, and there is no way we are not going there." So, I instructed him to call the factory and find out when we could visit. He arranged an appointment for the next morning, but told us the man indicated that he was all sold out for the season, but we should come just to meet him and see what he was all about.

Early the next morning, off we went to the very low rent district of Naples. When we arrived, Pietro made sure we took everything out of the car, as the locals were notorious for pilfering any autos that did not belong to "the neighborhood."

There we were walking up four flights to the factory, and Laura turned to me and said "sure, my mother is home baby sitting for our children and she thinks her daughter is being waltzed around only the finest places in Europe, and here I am skipping over dog leavings all over the steps in a Naples apartment house in the wrong section of town." We both chuckled, but proceeded up the last flight and finally arrived at the tortoise factory which turned out to be no more than a run down apartment in this squalor of a building, but the owner, Nino, did have a tiny showroom that consisted of one bench, one chair, one table and a wall full of drawers. (Obviously the "factory" was located elsewhere.)

Pietro explained to him who we were and what our mission was, and he told us he well understood our quest and our frustration up to now, as he believed he was indeed the only surviving purveyor of genuine tortoise jewelry in all of Italy and perhaps the world.

Now we really were excited as we had found "the holy grail" of tortoise jewelry and we could not wait to see what he had to show.

Nino carefully explained that he was sold out for the next six months, but he would give us an idea of what he supplied. With that, he took out a drawer filled with tortoise bangles of all widths and shades, ranging from dark brown to light amber.

He then proceeded to take out other drawers that were filled with tortoise beads, buttons, hoop earrings, links, and pins. By this time Laura and I were literally frothing at the mouth and instructed Pietro to ask him which pieces we could purchase. Nino reiterated that he was all sold out and his production was six months behind.

Now Laura swung in to gear. She asked Pietro to inform Nino of her Italian heritage, and that her grandmother was from Media de Sorrento and how could he refuse to sell us some of his pieces so we could at least test the American market? She smiled and oohed and aahed at every piece as she plunged into doing her best "Italian dance."

To make a long story short, an hour and a half later, EVERY piece of his tortoise collection was "in our tray" for delivery to us at the hotel in two days. Laura had worked her feminine Italian magic and we finally left and were all giddy from the "coup" we had just pulled off. (Either that or we had just been cleverly misled...... it mattered not!!!).

That evening before going to dinner, the first thing I did was to place an international call directly to Gloria Fiore at Bonwit Teller. When I related the story to her she said, "Bernard, buy every piece you can and it all belongs to me exclusively at Bonwit's." "We will run a full page ad in the NY. Times as soon as you return and can develop the tortoise parts into meaningful jewelry."

I estimated the collection to be about $25,000 with labor, shipping, & duty and she said "Bernard, I repeat, it is all mine and hurry home as I am very excited about this."

Laura and I then went out to celebrate with a lovely dinner in an upscale seafood restaurant overlooking the Bay of Naples.

The next morning I was going to arrange for a bank transfer so we would have the money to pay Nino upon delivery. Much to my dismay, it was a bank holiday in Italy, and I could not arrange to have a transfer in time for me to pay him the following morning.

I then called upon Roberto, the manager of the Excelsior that we had befriended on earlier visits, and asked if the hotel could give me a cash advance and put it on my bill which of course I would pay for with my credit card when we checked out the next day. He understood the situation, but Ciga hotel rules precluded him from advancing any more than $500 to any guest, but he took it upon himself to extend that to $ 500 for each of us so we ended up with $ 1,000, which was still about $4,000 short of what we were going to need, but it was what it was.

The following day, Nino showed up with the entire collection and placed it piece by piece on the bed in our suite so we could all review it and go over the prices. When we had finished that and we confirmed that we would be taking every piece he had bought, Pietro had the unpleasant task of informing Nino that because of the Italian banking holiday, I could only offer him $ 1,000, and the balance I would have to send from the States in a day or two, as this was our last stop of the trip.

He looked at Laura, then me, and then turned to Pietro and said "no problem as I trust these people," and he then proceeded to re wrap the goods and "hand them over" to us.

My god, what a leap of faith in us (actually in Laura, I am sure), and of course we were overwhelmed by his trust and the bundle of goods he then thrust at us.

I immediately went down to the lobby to speak to Roberto and request a vault box for the tortoise which was now in Laura's personal Vuitton satchel bag. He frowned and told me he had no facility, including the hotel safe, that he could offer me that evening and we would have to "keep it safely by our side," as he reminded me that after all, we were in Naples.

That evening, Laura and I stayed in, ordered room service, and slept with the tortoise between us in the bed......... I swear that is true!!!!!

The next morning, we were heading up to Rome for an overnight stay and then flying home to NY. the following morning, so I proceeded to head down to the lobby to settle the bill, and Laura was in charge of finishing the packing, which was our "standard operating procedure."

I settled up with the cashier, and asked the bellman to accompany me up to the room as we were ready to depart, and Pietro had the car waiting at the front entrance of the hotel.

The bags were placed in the trunk, and as we were preparing to leave I noticed the chamber maid, followed by the concierge and the doorman, come running out to us frantically flailing their arms and yelling in Italian. Following a few steps behind was my friend Roberto, the hotel manager. Everyone started talking in heated Italian to Pietro, and it was not until Roberto came over to me that I had any inkling of what was happening.

"Bernard," Roberto whispered, "we have a problem in that the chamber maid says the leather Ciga writing portfolio was not in the room when she entered it upon your departure. Since it is quite costly, her job is to immediately check for it when a guest checks out, as she is financially responsible for it if it is missing." She says it is missing!!!!!

Well, knowing my lovely wife's penchant for pretty things like that, I immediately turned to her and asked if she had taken it, and she said emphatically said "no." So naively, I turned to Roberto and said maybe we should go back up to the room and see if the maid "missed it." We did and of course it was not up there. I immediately knew then that Ms. Laura had purloined it, but would not admit to it.

So we want down to the car again and opened her suitcase and observed that it was not in there, and I said, "Laura should I open my suitcase?" (Which of course she had packed a few minutes ago back up in the room). She said "sure, but it would not be in there." So I opened the case and under a shirt or two, astoundingly, there was the writing portfolio which Laura said must have "fallen into the suitcase as she was packing up," and she just didn't notice it.

When I handed the portfolio over to Roberto, he smiled and asked me to please accompany him back to his office, where I expected him to read me the riot act.

Instead, after we were both seated in his office, he burst out laughing and told me this happens at least once a week, and to not feel embarrassed, which of course he knew I was. He then reached into a drawer behind him and took out a gift package and asked me to give it to Laura as a souvenir. I sheepishly took the packet, gave him a big hug and started out thru the lobby to the car, having to pass the doorman, concierge and maid all of whom smiled knowingly and wished me a good journey.

Obviously this was not the first time they had dealt with a lady taking the beautiful and expensive leather Ciga writing portfolio as a souvenir. It certainly took up less space than a bath towel or robe.

I was thoroughly mortified at "stealing" from the very manager who was kind enough to advance me $ 1,000 just the day before, so I was scowling when I got in to the car and told Pietro to get the hell out of Naples as fast as we could.

I said not a word for about five minutes, wanting Laura to stew a little, as she had no idea what Roberto had said to me in his office, and I truly wanted her to suffer as I had when we "discovered" the portfolio in my bag.

I finally burst out laughing and Pietro and Laura soon followed my lead and we laughed our way out of Naples. Laura was really taken aback when I gave her the memento that Roberto had given me for her, and it turned out to be a lovely Ciga silk scarf with the Ciga logo, which she promptly flung around her neck and we all continued laughing almost all the way to Rome.

We checked into the Grand Hotel for the night, and Pietro promised us a great meal at Alfredo's the fine restaurant he had been the maître' d at for many years prior to becoming a driver.

Upon our arrival, he was warmly welcomed, and as soon as we were seated a heavily mustached Alfredo appeared to meet, greet and sit with us, and of course the main dining feature was a huge portion of fettuccine Alfredo.

The next morning, Pietro, drove us to the airport and kissed us goodbye and told us he had never had a three week adventure like the one he had just experienced. He wanted to know when we were planning our next trip as he wanted to remain available, and we told him to sit tight and let us see what happens with all the goods we had just purchased.

We were due to land in NYC around 3PM on a Wednesday afternoon and Laura was busy filling out the customs form on the plane as we approached JFK and she turned to me and said "hey let us list the tortoise jewelry as plastic as it certainly looks like it and then we can "reduce the cost price of the goods for customs purposes." I looked at her and said emphatically, "We will claim it for what it is, genuine tortoise jewelry, but you can reduce the cost price to under $ 1, 000," which she did.

Upon landing, the tortoise and other jewelry samples we had claimed were "held" by customs as commercial samples in excess of $500 had to be cleared by your licensed and registered customs broker.

The next day I went into the office & Laura went back to JFK to meet with our customs broker and to clear the shipment which she then personally drove in to NYC. Once I had the goods in my possession, I immediately called Gloria Fiore of Bonwit Teller and made a date for her to come down the next day to review the assortment and let us know how she would like us to manipulate the beads and parts into a full blown collection for her ad and presentation a month or two down the road.

A month later, Les Bernard delivered the entire collection, invoiced at about $27,500, to Bonwit Teller who then later ran a full page Sunday ad in the New York

Times (which Les Bernard participated in to the tune of $ 3,750). The reaction was explosive, and Gloria called me to re order as much tortoise from Italy as I could, so I immediately telexed to Pietro (there was no fax or computers back then) to contact Nino and to repeat our entire order for shipment ASAP.

The very next day, at about noon, I received a frantic call From Gloria informing me that the U.S. Fish and Wildlife service was in the store threatening to close down the entire 5th ave Bonwit Teller unless they immediately removed all the illegal tortoise from the store, as it was on the Endangered Species List.

I was more than just a little shocked as neither Gloria nor I had any knowledge of the Fish and Wildlife Service or that tortoise was on an endangered list of any kind.

That evening on the 6 o'clock news there was a story on how the government had barnstormed Bonwit Teller, Henri Bendel, and Cartier and had confiscated all the tortoise that they had in their stores, and that they were planning on approaching the importer (to the Bonwit operation) Les Bernard Inc. I noted that at least we were being mentioned in good company.

The following day, two Fish and Wildlife agents visited my showroom and confiscated all the samples that remained on our shelf as they had done with the entire inventory Bonwit Teller had in the show cases at the store. They then asked for my attorneys name and number as the District Attorney would probably want to speak to us and him about this incident.

Two days later I received word from my business attorney, Harry Metrick, that he had received the anticipated call from the DA's office and that we were to appear to discuss the matter. When I related to him that I was in the middle of market week and would not be able to make it, he suggested that Laura make the appearance on behalf of the firm, as he knew she was "cool under pressure."

He added that he just wanted me to know that he would not be accompanying her to the DA's office, but rather his partner Sy Ostrow would, as he was a criminal attorney, and this was indeed classified as a criminal matter, as the DA was approaching this as an act of smuggling.

It was at this point that I started "to sweat" as the seriousness of the offense and the possible penalties of a hefty fine and prison time would be on the table. Laura of course was happy to go, and she told me this would be "duck soup" for her as she would just wear a short skirt and a tight fitting sweater and would sweet talk the DA.

So on June 10th she went downtown to meet Sy for a quick briefing as he wanted to import the seriousness of the matter to her lest she be too flippant in her approach. They arrived at the DA's office in time to see Gloria Fiore exiting the office with a concerned smile as she greeted Laura and Sy and then left the building.

It was now Laura's turn, and as she entered the office she realized to her shock and dismay that the assistant DA handling the case was a woman not a man, so there went her short skirt and tight sweater "defense" right out the window. The DA asked Sy where I was. He and Laura explained that it was market week and that I was extremely busy with customers, and that she was fully authorized to be deposed on the company's behalf, especially since she had filled out the customs forms and was quite familiar with the entire scenario.

When the DA told her they were looking at this as a case of smuggling prohibited materials into the country, Laura responded, "wait just a minute, we had no intention of smuggling anything into the country and if you refer to our customs entry form and brokers release, we clearly indicated that this was genuine tortoise, and we even discussed that with the customs agent who never indicated to us that the product was illegal."

The young sharp female DA responded "Mrs. Shapiro, you and your husband are importers of assorted jewelry and raw materials, and it is therefore your duty and obligation to know the laws. The customs agents are not responsible for allowing illegal products in to the country." "You, as the importer, bear that responsibility, and you "should have known."

However, having said that, she noted that during her interview with the buyer of Bonwit Teller, she had indeed admitted to encouraging you to "find genuine tortoise jewelry" on your trip and she showed us the full page ad, "which has convinced us that you were not trying to hide anything, but rather acted imprudently and with lack of knowledge, so we are not going to pursue criminal charges against you." "However, from the invoices Bonwit showed us, and the customs declaration you presented upon entering the country, it appears that you made a very handsome profit on this transaction, and we will therefore consider a significant civil fine to be levied." At this point Laura indicated that not only will we be refunding the entire invoice amount to Bonwit Teller, but we will also still have to pay our portion of the cost of the NY Times ad, so that we have already been punished financially. The DA said she would take all of that into consideration when making her decision.

Two weeks later we learned that the DA had decided to just put Les Bernard on probation regarding the importation of raw materials from abroad. There would be no civil fine levied, or any criminal charges be brought, as the determination was that we were ignorant of the laws and had no malicious intent, since we had declared the product properly at the point of entering the country. Laura and I spent many hours talking about what would have happened if we had declared the goods as "plastic beads and parts" as she wanted to do. Oh my God, one or both of us would have ended up in jail, and with a substantial fine, so this was one of those occasions when my adamancy was a saving grace.

The matter was closed and Gloria, Laura and I celebrated with a casual dinner at our home as we both had learned a valuable lesson.

As a post script to the story, and you would have to have known Laura to appreciate this, the following year when we were in Naples to buy coral, Laura indicated that she wanted to visit Nino again as she had no tortoise jewelry to show for all of our efforts. I told her she was crazy and if we did go and she did get some bangles, and other objects of tortoise, that she could "clear customs by herself," as this time as we were "on notice." Well of course we went, and she bought and wore the darn bangles right thru customs with no problems and to this day my daughters have some very rare tortoise bangles.

That is the whole truth and nothing but the truth!!!

HONG KONG AND THE CANTON FAIR
IN MAINLAND CHINA

It was October of 1974 when we first traveled to Asia as a result of our invitation to attend the Canton Trade Fair in Mainland China. Nixon has just opened up trade and tourism with the Mainland, and the Chinese "Dragon Lady" I had met in Montreal the previous summer, had made good on her promise to have Les Bernard invited to the fair as soon as it was permissible.

Since we were planning on first visiting Taiwan, the Republic of China, we were informed that in order to enter Mainland China, the Peoples Republic of China, we would need a "clean second passport," as the Mainland would not let us enter if there was any evidence of us having visited Taiwan. I inquired of the State Department if this was possible, and was surprised how easy it was to obtain that second "clean" passport by just showing a copy of our invitation to the Canton Fair.

In Taipei we discovered a wonderful resource for abalone shell beads and parts, and in the years to come Taiwan was always on our itinerary as abalone was an extremely well received product back in the states.

We arrived in Hong Kong in mid October as the Canton Fair was scheduled to open on the 15th as it did every April and October. You must remember the rest of the world had been doing business with China for many years and the Americans were the "new kids on the block" so to speak. We had to obtain a travel visa to China which we applied for in Hong Kong. In the three days it took to receive the visa, we started to shop the local ivory market. We did in fact locate a couple of seemingly "with it" ivory sources and one, Wing Fung Arts, came to visit us at the Peninsula Hotel and we placed a rather small opening order for some of their designs that appealed to us. This company turned out to be our most significant and reliable ivory resource for the ensuing years.

On the day we were to travel into Mainland, we boarded a train at the Star Ferry terminal along with a few other Americans, one of whom had been to the Mainland before, but for the rest of us, it was our initial exposure to this part of the world and the train was really the only available means of travel for this initial trip.

Sitting next to us was a vice president of a mid west oil company and his Asian agent. We were in the middle of chatting with them when the conductor on the train came over and informed the agent that he had to move to another car, as the one we were in was reserved for Westerners. The Americans were all shocked that here in Asia, there was discrimination against an Asian, but he seemed to understand, and he did in fact move.

About an hour and a half later, the train stopped at the border of Mainland and we were informed that we all had to disembark and take our luggage to customs where it would be inspected while we were to be served lunch. While sitting at this extremely large round table with the other Americans, we started to chat with the father and son team that had previously visited the Mainland and had ordered a thousand sheepskin coats which they had already received back in the States. They explained to us that the coats had arrived with the zippers mounted in a contrasting color to the actual jackets which rendered them unsalable in the American market. They indicated that the Chinese could not understand the problem as the zippers worked just fine, and no one had told them the zipper borders had to coordinate with the color of the jackets. The lesson to be learned here was that "you buy what you see" and you did not, at least at this early stage, try to change any of their styles. To avoid any problems, we needed to restrict our purchases to what we saw, not what we wished to create.

After a great Chinese lunch, we were ushered back in to the customs area and Laura and I were questioned at great length, as they wanted to know where Laura's watch was, since she was not wearing one on her wrist. We tried to explain that she did not bring a watch with her on this trip, but they just could not seem to accept that, and were obviously concerned that she was hiding it on her person, and inferred that it was to be used as a bribe to anyone we might end up doing business with. They finally realized that she did not have a watch either on her person or in her luggage, and we were then allowed to re board the trains for the one hour ride to Canton.

I can still remember the look on Laura's face when she returned from the train's "ladies room" as it was her first experience with an eastern toilet which was basically a hole in the floor upon which she had to squat. Laura who was usually so cool about things, was clearly a little unsettled about the plumbing facilities she may likely encounter for the rest of our trip.

When we arrived in Canton (now re named Kwangchow) the Westerners were greeted and ushered into one of three cars waiting at the station. All non Westerners were either met by friends with bicycles, or started to walk to wherever they were going as there were no other cars in sight. It was a very different time those thirty nine years ago, and we quickly learned that it was a bicycle society with the limited automobiles reserved for government officials or visiting Westerners.

All the Americans that we traveled with were driven to the Tung Fang Hotel which was located across the street from the Fair grounds. If the name of the hotel puts you off, I can assure you it was appropriately titled as it was certainly not a five star hotel, and had none of the amenities we are all used to. Those of us who were traveling with another person were escorted to our rooms and those that were traveling alone were then "matched up" with another single traveler as there was no such thing as a private single room.

Now I must say, we had received some forewarnings of what to expect in Mainland, but the little information we had received in no way prepared us for the shock of our overnight accommodations. When we entered our room the most outstanding detail were the two enormous mosquito nets, one over each bed, which kind of told us what to expect, but fortunately Laura had listened to her pre travel info and had bought footy PJ's for this two night stay. We were informed that the room rate was the equivalent of US. $11 per night and Laura immediately said, upon seeing our room. that it was the most overpriced hotel room she had ever stayed in. The water from the tap was brownish and cold and the bath towels hanging on hooks were more the size of what we would call a wash cloth. Showering was a waste and we just rinsed off each morning and evening. She did manage to sleep in the room during the first night, but the second night she spent on one of the lobby couches.

Breakfast was an international scene with business visitors from all over the world, yet just a small handful of Americans, as this was the very first Fair that we could attend, and I doubted if there were more than a ½ dozen of us that had received timely invitations. We learned the hard way that it would be best to be first at breakfast as the tablecloths remained for the entire morning, so if you wanted a "clean" setting, you needed to be early at the table.

I will say the hotel was most convenient, as it was directly across the street from the pavilion entrance. The very first thing we noticed as we made our way to the jewelry section were large TV boxes stacked along the walls and they all said MADE IN TAIWAN. You could not visit the Mainland if your passport had a Taiwan entry in it, but for sure if you were at the Fair you could purchase merchandise made in Taiwan. Here was a prime example of the hypocrisy we all endure in the politics vs. business world we reside in.

When we finally arrived at the jewelry section, we were treated to the specter of three rather large rooms all surrounded by shelves with an assortment of semi precious nugget necklaces in rose quartz, tiger eye, sodalite, turquoise, topaz, and an array of cloisonné beads and parts. This semi precious trove occupied two of the three rooms with the last one consisting of 14 K jewelry and cultured pearls which were of no real interest to us.

We were introduced to our contact person who spoke fluent English and explained to us that we were dealing directly with a government owned factory and whatever we saw was immediately available (no more and no less), and we were free to roam the rooms with him and select whatever we wished, and at the conclusion of our buying, a contract would be written to cover our purchase. Well, we had a ball selecting every semi precious nugget necklace we could find and we ended up purchasing every one they had to offer. We then "took a shot" with a few thousand cloisonné beads and bangles, not knowing what the reaction would be back home to this intricate and costly method of enameling.

In the early evening of the first day at the fair, we were treated to a car ride around the city. You must remember there were at most maybe six cars that we saw as everyone traveled by bicycle and the sight of thousands of people on bikes was something to behold. Soon, we heard some wonderful oriental music emanating from behind a large wall adjacent to the road. When I asked the driver where the music was coming from he said "from the drive in movie on the other side of the wall." He drove us around the wall and there standing watching the big screen, were hundreds of Chinese, holding on to their bicycles. Yes it was an outdoor drive in movie, but there were no people sitting in cars, just standing next to their bikes. A sight to behold!!!

That evening, I invited the other Americans to join us for a dinner outside of the hotel at a recommended restaurant about two blocks away. We were assured it was more than safe to go and come as there was no petty crime here, since if you were caught stealing you had either a finger (s) or hand cut off, depending on the severity of the offense.

We turned out to be ten and we all enjoyed a truly gourmet Chinese meal while trading our "war" stories from the days experiences. When I picked up the bill I was shocked by the total of $ 25 including a tip for all ten of us or about $ 2.50 a person.

Let us remember it was 1974 and this was really the first contingent of Westerners they had experienced. I gladly paid the bill and we all walked back on unlit streets to our wonderful Tung Fang Hotel.

The second evening we were informed that the Fair officials had arranged a special meal for the ten of us and they escorted us (by car) to a lovely restaurant where we were led to a private roof top dining area.

They started off with soup and when the bird's head was dropped into Laura's bowl I thought she would pass out, but it turns out she was the designated guest of honor and the bird's head was reserved for her. She did not eat it, nor did any of us partake when dog or snake were offered

On the last morning we were at the Fair, we were taken into a room for our contract signing. To avoid any shipping complications, we directed that the jewelry be sent down to Hong Kong where our Chinese lady friend had offered to prepare the goods properly for re shipment to the States.

Everything would be done by a letter of credit that adhered to the terms of sale. All of this was "negotiated" over tea and ultra politeness by all of the government employees, but realistically the protocol was set by the government and there was no room for any deviation or negotiation.

Later that afternoon, we were on the train en route to our luxurious room at the Peninsula Hotel in Hong Kong, and of course the first thing we did was jump into a hot fifteen minute shower and go down to Gadi's for a Western style meal. It was so nice to be back in our comfort zone, but we both recognized the significance of the trip and we were very excited about all that we had "discovered."

We met the next day with our Chinese lady friend who through her company was handling the trans shipment of our semi precious and cloisonné "finds." Her main business was in oil so this was just a matter of fun for her, as the dollars represented were miniscule compared to her real business.

Although Nixon had "opened" up trade, China was still a "non favored nation" when it came to import duties so the potential charges on any finished goods we bought was a 110% on top of the original cost. Hence the bargain $ 9.00 semi precious necklaces would cost us, with air freight, landed in the U.S. approximately $21.00 which made it no longer "a bargain." Since the duty rate on unfinished goods was just 10%, I suggested that our Chinese friend have her staff cut up the knotted beaded necklaces and place the loose beads in a plastic bag with the clasp and that my staff in NY. would re string and re knot the necklaces at a fraction of the cost. She looked at me in amazement and said that was a great idea and she gave us a price of .50 per necklace which meant the landed cost (not including shipping etc) would be about $ 11 not $ 21 which was a huge savings which we in turn could pass on to our retail clients back home.

All of our subsequent shipments were routed thru her company and we never had a problem with any of the goods we imported from the Mainland. This was due in part to the fact that I had listened to the father-son team who told me to buy only what I saw and not be creative. We of course had the liberty and ability of re designing any of the products once they were in my factory at home, so this rule of thumb was followed in all the ensuing shipments.

During our second sojourn to the next Fair, we kept our room at the Peninsula and told the house boy not to be alarmed as we were taking two pillows, and sheets and towels with us to Canton, and would bring them back upon our return. This mollified Laura and made our sleeping arrangements a bit more tolerable.

After three such trips, China Airlines started daily service from Hong Kong to Canton, enabling us to fly in early in the morning, shop at the Fair, and take the last flight out, and be back in Hong Kong for dinner, and this is exactly how we handled our last few trips into the Mainland.

We stopped attending the Fair a few years later as we started to notice the buyers from Bloomingdales, Saks 5th and other customers of ours, sitting next to us in the semi precious room, so we knew it was just a matter of time that all the large retailers would be sending their buyers in to do business directly. It was just the way it was. We had a great six year exclusive run, and in the fashion business that was more than you could expect.

We had the distinct pleasure of visiting the Mainland, prior to the advent of five star accommodations, credit cards, and international phone availability. It was a time before China emerged and was accessible to the West and it was a fabulous experience. We did return in the early 90's on vacation with our friends and went directly to Peking, (now Beijing) where we stayed in the White Swan five star hotel, with in room phones, direct dialing to the States, and the use of credit cards, and a car and driver at our disposal. Fifteen years or so made a world of difference, and we were so lucky to have experienced "the old China" which was so unlike anything we had ever been exposed to.

Although our business eventually dwindled with the Mainland, we did continue to import cloisonné beads and parts that we were able to manipulate into uniquely designed necklaces and pendants in our NY. facility. We did, however, return to Hong Kong twice annually, making over twenty four such trips, as ivory became our most important semi precious product over the years, and was the subject of at least ½ dozen full page color ads in Vogue, Harpers or Elle, until it too was placed on the endangered species list.

Hong Kong was then still a British protectorate and a most tantalizing city for both our business and for Laura's shopping for the kids. It was a metropolis that pulsated the minute you exited Kai Tak airport and into the Rolls Royce taking you to the Peninsula or the Regent. It was an exciting and wonderful time for us both and we did manage to expose Blair and Brie to Asia on two trips. Again, the business had afforded us the luxury of traveling, experiencing different cultures, and widening the exposure of two Bronx born babies.

INDIA & GOOD MORNING HONG KONG
circa 1984-86

Laura and I made a conscious effort to avoid doing business in India as we had heard so many unsettling stories about people becoming very ill from the food, and the squalor we would have to behold, so we decided we just did not want to subject ourselves to any possible health issues or observe inhumane conditions. However, we started to receive numerous retailers' requests for hand made brass beads and bangles and the best sources for that were indeed in Delhi, so we finally succumbed to making the trip.

We arrived aboard our Pan Am flight at 1AM local time and walked into a contingent of armed soldiers that were stationed through out the airport and its surroundings. It was scary arriving in the middle of the night with gun bearing security everywhere, but thankfully, we never did experience any problems entering, doing business, or leaving the country.

I had heard that uncovering reliable sources in India was problematic so I did some research and made contact with an American agent that was residing in Delhi. I arranged to have him accompany us to recommended manufacturers, and thereafter to monitor the progress of the manufacturing and shipping of any goods we purchased. He had alerted us to bring canned foods with us and he cautioned us not to eat at any restaurants outside of the Oberoi Hotel where we were staying. The very first morning he picked us up he showed us the lunch he had brought for us, and it was wrapped in newspaper as he claimed that was the most sanitary means available. Whenever we visited a resource he would not let us drink any liquids unless he himself opened the bottles or boiled the water for tea. We followed his lead and never suffered any food related illness during our multiple visits. After two days, Laura and I were delighted that we had made the trip as here, once more, we really experienced a very different culture and way of life. Visiting old Delhi with all the vendors lining the streets and the sight of cows roaming among us was mind boggling, but the maimed professional beggars were indeed quite unsettling.

We also managed a day trip to over crowded Bombay, but never found the time to visit the Taj Mahal. Shame on us that we never took a day off to visit this site in the town of Agra. We always said we would do it on our next trip, but that never happened.

We returned to Delhi one more time for business and en route to our first stop in Bangkok, where we were told we would find amazing artifacts to convert into fashion jewelry.

The Alitalia flight to Bangkok departed Delhi at 2AM and we were booked in Super First Class. Neither of us had a clue as to what that was, but it turned out for a small supplement we were ushered upstairs in a 747 which had only six seats and two flight attendants. Yes it was indeed a special first class with an abundance of interesting food, but at 2AM we really did nothing but sleep until our arrival in Bangkok early that morning.

Upon entering a taxi to our hotel, the driver asked us why we would be coming to Thailand in the midst of a revolution? With a flourish, he flung the local newspaper into the back of the cab with a picture on the front page (in red) of tanks entering the city. We were stunned and apprehensive, but somewhat calmed upon arriving at the Intercontinental Hotel when the desk clerk informed us that it was a "bloodless" coup and we would not encounter any problems, but we did need to observe the evening curfew. Needless to say we were somewhat relieved, but we really had no plans on leaving the hotel in the evenings as again we were warned to eat all our meals there.

We found very little to purchase in Bangkok except for ancient shards of pottery that were mounted in silver settings and used for pendants. What I did find was a severe case of food poisoning that landed me in bed for two days (in spite of the fact that we never ate outside of the hotel).

I was "rescued" by the American lady we were buying the jewelry from as she came to the hotel and promised me if I took the pill she was giving me, which truly was the size of a small meatball, that I would be better the next day.

I was desperate and took her at her word and it did cure me so we could "get out of town" ASAP en route to our next stop which was Hong Kong. We never returned to Bangkok for business, but we did visit briefly a few years later with Blair and Brie for a mini vacation during one of our numerous Hong Kong buying trips. Although aesthetically intriguing, it was really the only city that we visited that did not offer us a substantial business incentive to return.

Based on Les Bernard's overwhelming success on the European trade show circuit, I decided to take a leap of faith and sign up for the Hong Kong Accessory Trade Fair. In the prior years, our Hong Kong trips concentrated on Ivory, but that business was now non existent due to the designation of Ivory as an endangered species so it was strictly a "selling trip."

When I registered at the Fair, I was given a note asking me to please come down to the public relations office as soon as I had completed setting up my display booth. Laura and I were a little perplexed as we had no idea what the PR department wanted with Les Bernard.

As it turned out, they wanted to know if I was willing to appear on the next mornings edition of "Good Morning Hong Kong," and they went on to explain that we were the very first American accessory company to display at the show, and they thought it newsworthy and of interest to upscale Asian retailers.

Laura turned white and said to me, "you can not go on TV!!! Suppose they ask you questions that you can not answer?" I replied, "If their questions are about Les Bernard's fashion jewelry and why we are here, I doubt if there is any question that I can not answer totally and honestly."

The next morning at 5AM we were picked up in a limousine and whisked off to the TV studio and promptly seated in the "green room." Thereafter, out came a very attractive Asian lady who would be interviewing me and she proceeded to fill me in on what she was going to discuss and the questions she would be asking. She took my samples with her and that was the last I saw of her until I was ushered on to the set of "Good Morning Hong Kong" some 30 minutes later at about 8 AM.

After being led thru all the wires and cables I was seated on a couch and there in front of me on a large coffee table were the Les Bernard samples. She then introduced me and started to ask me questions as to why I was in Hong Kong trying to sell to South East Asia, when indeed many of the raw materials Les Bernard was using, did in fact originate from the region.

I explained the importance of creative styling utilizing the beautiful stones and parts that we had purchased from the region, and that we felt the jewelry would be well received because of the originality of the designs that utilized those indigenous materials.

She then turned to the camera and started to repeat everything I said, BUT in Chinese to the local audience. This I was not expecting, but I was cool and the interview lasted about fifteen minutes at the conclusion of which, I was guided back to the green room where Laura had been nervously watching the interview on the screen. She thought I had excelled, but she was glad to be out of there, and she doubted if anyone of note would have seen this early morning interview.

It was now 8:30 AM in Hong Kong and we were driven directly to the fair that opened at 9.

Much to our very pleasant surprise, the very first ½ dozen or so visitors to our booth smiled at me and said "I saw you on TV this morning and that is why I am here."

We did eventually develop some business in S.E. Asia with a few leading upscale boutiques in both Hong Kong and Singapore, but it never approached the success of our European market.

It was worth it just for the experience and of course I had my fifteen minutes of fame.

My only regret is not requesting a tape of the interview as I have no record of the TV station, nor the identity of the lovely early morning anchor lady.

From 1974- 1992, we made over two dozen trips to Southeast Asia, which included:

Mainland China (Canton) for semi precious nuggets and cloisonné beads and bangles.

The Philippines (Cebu City) where we purchased mostly shell and mother of pearl products

Taiwan, (Taipei) where we bought abalone shell and a multitude of genuine jade beads, bangles and pendant parts.

Thailand (Bangkok), where we selected ancient shards that we mounted in the States and sold as pendants. (The least productive city for our jewelry needs).

Japan (Osaka), where we dealt exclusively with faux cultured round and irregular shaped Biwa pearls and hand made glass beads in tones of apple jade, lavender jade, and angel skin coral.

India (Delhi), where we purchased brass bangles and beads and products made of antiqued bone.

And of course in Hong Kong where we designed and purchased the lovely Ivory creations for which we became well known.

We had an amazing twenty five year journey and were extremely lucky to see parts of the world that very few are afforded the opportunity to experience, and that is why I repeatedly say to this day that our lives were governed a great deal by our travel odyssey.

My all time cutest at four — 1940

I am already nautically inclined at six -- 1942

With my mom at the Raleigh Hotel Pool—*South Beach*, Miami—1944

The Bar Mitzvah boy and guests at the New Yorker Hotel 1949

The Swimmer and the start of the race – 1952

Gryphon, the Senior Men's Honor Society—Clark University—1956
Paul and I are second and third from the right

My Olds convertible-- journey across America—Berthoud Pass, Colorado 1957

Mom and Dad on their 30 ft. Ulrichsen sea skiff—circa 1953

Laura's graduation--- Naval Officers School , Newport, R.I--. 1965

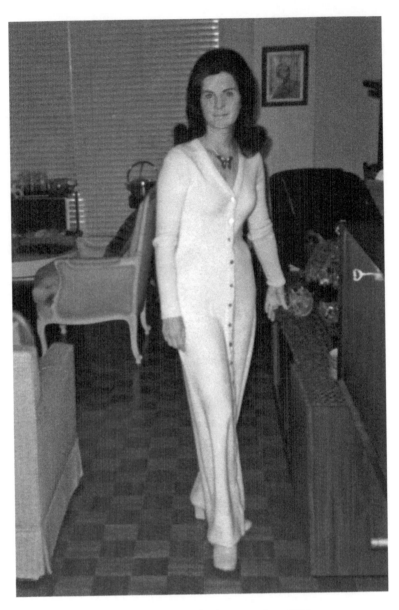

Laura in our New York. Apartment-- 1971

Laura at the Chanticleer Inn, Sconset, Nantucket Island -- 1973
the very day she learned she was pregnant with Blair

Laura's mom with Blair -- 1974

Laura's dad with D'artagnan—1974

The brothers D'artagnan and Brandeis – 1975

Brie with Moose, the gentle giant – 1980

At Alfredo's with Pietro and his family – circa 1978

Larry and Gemma's mountain top palazzo, Durazanno, Italy-- 1980

Blair and Brie in the front courtyard of Ambiance—1981

Laura at Sloans Curve in Palm Beach—1987

Laura and Blair at Lauren's wedding -- 1987

Lauren and Larry at their wedding in Palm Beach—1987

Elissa with her Akita, Montana—1988

Madonna with her body guard—Hotel Du Cap-- Cap Antibes, France—1988

Opening day of 1st Muffin Lady Diet Emporium, Laura and Joyce-1990

Laura, Blair and Brie, St. Martin—1992

Staying in shape at the La Samanna gym -- 1992

With Laura St. Martin.—1992

Chop Stix- our first Shar- Pei – 1993

White Water rafting with the poker guys-- Colorado River. 1994

Filling in the divots at the polo matches @ Old Westbury L.I. 1994

$25*

This Flower Opens

new vistas in mobile jewelry—growing, at a touch, from a tightly closed bud to a fullblown 2″ flower pin with glitter-paved center to match the petals. And each petal twists individually as well, for a myriad of different shapes. By Les Bernard. In golden color metal paved with rhinestones, simulated emerald, ruby, sapphire or light topaz glitter. Also in silvery color paved with rhinestones. $25*

On mail or phone orders, add 25c beyond delivery area.
*Plus 10% Fed. tax

*Costume Jewelry,
Street Floor*

BERGDORF GOODMAN
5 th AVE. at 58th ST. NEW YORK 19
ON THE PLAZA

First ad on Les Bernard Jewelry -- Bergdorf Goodman   August, 1964
The patented moveable petal flower pin

Out of the Blue

. . . simulated baroque pearls in a brand-new color that creates beautifully luminous lighting effects against any costume shade. Each large pearly bead looks as if it had been dipped in a blue haze, reflecting back soft glimmers of the color it is worn with. Styled by Les Bernard, we show a single strand long necklace, $16.50*, a double strand short necklace, $21*, and matching earrings, $5*. Not shown: single strand short necklace, $12*; double strand long necklace, $29*.

On mail or phone orders, add 25c beyond delivery area.
*Plus 10% Fed. tax

Costume Jewelry,
Street Floor

5th AVE. at 58th ST. NEW YORK 19
ON THE PLAZA

Second ad on Les Bernard Jewelry—Bergdorf Goodman. September, 1964
Twilight Blue Pearls

Lavender branch coral—a Les Bernard exclusive—Vogue ad   1980

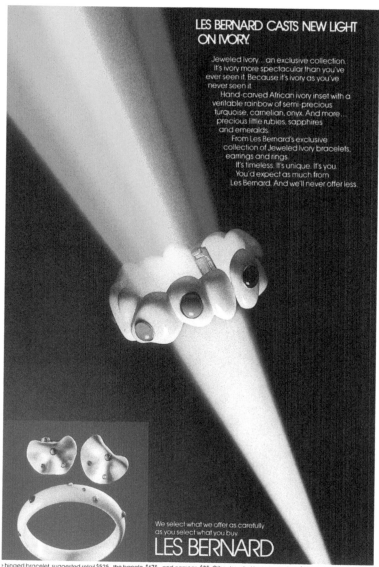
Genuine Ivory with Precious and semi precious stones- -Vogue ad 1982

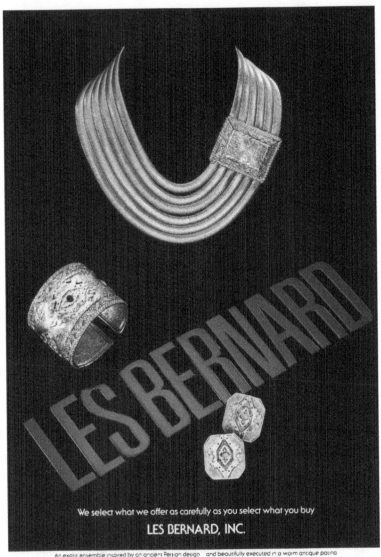

Persian gold chains -- Vogue ad   1984

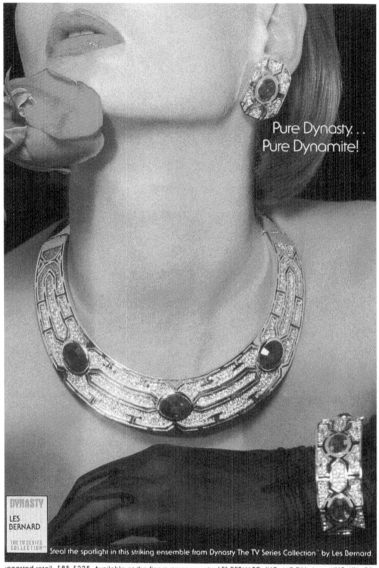

Pure Dynasty...
Pure Dynamite!

The Dynasty for T.V. collection by Les Bernard—Vogue ad 1985

Ambiance , Muttontown house, pool, cabana, green house , dog run , cottage—1976

Mirabelle, our St.Martin home—before the garden filled in -- 2001

Bernie's yacht at our dock in St. Martin--2007

Brie, Todd and Mayor Murcott -- exchanging wedding vows –2005

Brie and Todd with his parents, Martha and Peter Kraska—2005

Blair, Brie, Marley and Luca in Easthampton L.I.   2010

Marley and Luca fishing at Big Wolf in the Adirondacks -- 2011

CRASHING THE PLAZA WEDDING - 1992

Circa 1992 our dear friends Randy and Sue Jones were just finishing renovating the home they had purchased at the intersection of Chicken Valley Road and Rt. 107 in Brookville, NY, which was about a five minute ride from our house.

We had been friends for a few years and we both enjoyed casual dining and the local movies, and we were used to calling each other "last minute" and saying " hey if you are free let's go to Stangos for a meatball and spaghetti dinner" or the Old Brookville Diner for "pot luck" and that is just what we did. It was always spur of the moment, totally spontaneous, and we both enjoyed that kind of relationship.

So it was a great shock to them when Laura and I suggested that we were stagnating in what our social lives had morphed into, and how about if we arranged for a surprise planned day or evening with one couple taking charge on one Saturday night and the next month the other couple could reciprocate? We agreed that the spending limit would be no more than $250 as we were not intending to travel to Tahiti but rather locally.

A flip of the coin dictated that they "go first" and we were instructed to dress nicely, but casually, for our first surprise outing.

Randy came by to pick us up in his vintage Rolls Royce and insisted we sit in the rear, as he was chauffeuring us to our destination, which turned out to be in the middle of the Planting Fields Arboretum. There, Sue had prepared a lovely picnic lunch using her finest silver and crystal, and we were served magnificent champagne to accompany our goodies. It seems that through a friend, she had managed to secure permission to "have a picnic in the park," which was heretofore strictly forbidden. It was lovely and we thoroughly enjoyed it.

They then chauffeured us to the Old Westbury polo field where they had secured box seats for a lively polo match, which included stomping on the field during intermission and filling up the divots. It was a gas and again something we had never experienced.

To top it all off we then were taken to dinner at Buckram Stables in Locust Valley where the booths were built to resemble horse stalls. It was a fitting conclusion to our picnic, polo matches, and first mystery outing.

It was now our turn and we thought for quite a while to come up with an equalizer.

We took Randy and Sue to a gourmet cooking class on the Upper East Side of NYC, where we participated, with two other couples, in drinking cocktails, and preparing and then eating some wonderful pizza as that and a diet Pepsi were Randy's favorite kind of meal. Pizza and soda or meatballs and spaghetti. That was gourmet dining to Randy. We had a great time and were all properly sloshed by the end of the session.

We then took them over to the West Side to attend "Aunt Sylvia's Funeral," an off Broadway show that was a mock Jewish funeral, and it was hysterical, especially since Randy and Sue were very not Jewish, so it was all "news to them." We all laughed our collective asses off as we headed back to Long Island.

The following month it was their turn again and they really bowled us over with this one. Firstly, they asked if they could "borrow" our handy man, Harry, and to have him drive us down to Philadelphia where they had secured VIP passes for a showing of the "impressionists" at the Barnes Foundation. They knew that would really appeal to Laura. Upon our arrival, they sent the driver home, and when we inquired how we were getting back to NYC they refused to give us an immediate answer. At about 5:30 PM they rushed us by cab to the Amtrak Station in Philadelphia and we boarded a train directly to Madison Square Garden where we had center court seats for a Knick game, as Randy knew that would really appeal to me. (Just want to mention that they went over the budget by quite a bit which opened up the flood gates for us).

Now four weeks later, we had to come up with a topper and we were hard pressed to surpass the Philadelphia trip, but then Laura said "how about crashing a N.Y. wedding." I said "are you crazy?" Of course the answer was a resounding "yes," and the ball was placed in my court to make the arrangements.

I distinctly remember sitting in my office and calling the Plaza Hotel in NYC and speaking to the catering manager. I told him we were planning an affair for our daughter, and we wished to experience a Jewish wedding at the Plaza so she could get to see if that is what she really desired.

He said "no problem, come on in on November 17th when the Nachman (fictitious name) wedding with three hundred guests will take place and we could observe it all from beginning to end." He also indicated he would join us to answer any questions, but of course I had no intention of re contacting him as he had already, unknowingly, given me all the information I needed.

So after discussing it with Laura we agreed to proceed. She then called Sue and told her we were planning a special night in NYC, but that we had to first attend a wedding as one of my important customer's daughters was getting married that same night. We would have to make a courtesy appearance for the wedding ceremony and cocktail hour, but then we could take off to have our night of surprise fun.

Laura informed them that Randy would have to be "black tie" and Sue was to get all gussied up and wear every piece of jewelry she owned as this was going to be a full blown Jewish Plaza wedding and to "pull out all the stops." We added that they had to bring an overnight bag with jeans, shirts and sweaters for "the after wedding mystery night activities."

We picked them up at around 5 PM at their Brookville home, on a Saturday night in a stretch limo driven by our regular limo driver, Claude, who was "in" on the prank. We had champagne and caviar in the car and Sue and Randy were dressed "appropriately." Sue had taken Laura literally and was wearing just about every important piece of jewelry from her wardrobe.

By the time we arrived at the Plaza we were all a little "high" from the champagne and we were all ready to "party."

Upon disembarking from the limo we proceeded up the front steps and all of a sudden a voice rang out "Bernard" and over came another Bernard, the general manager of La Samanna in St. Martin who was also in black tie. He embraced both Laura and me, and we introduced him to Randy and Sue who just assumed he was another wedding attendee.

Upon walking in, we told them he was also from the bride's side, when the truth was that it was just a coincidence that he was there and in black tie, as he was attending another affair at the hotel, but it sure appeared as if Laura and I knew some of the family members.

Upon arriving at the reception area adjacent to the chapel, we all noticed a rather large round table with all the place cards lined up in alphabetical order, and when Sue asked if she should retrieve our cards, we both said no and "explained" that at a Jewish wedding it was really rude to retrieve the place cards prior to the actual ceremony. Whew, a disaster averted.

After some welcoming champagne, we followed the crowd into the chapel and took seats about midway in the room and the procession started almost immediately. Laura was two seats in off of the aisle and then me next to her and then Sue and then Randy. As soon as the procession started Laura whispered to the gentleman on her left, that she would be grateful if he could identify the family members as they came down the aisle, which he discreetly did. After each approached, Laura would turn to the three of us and announce "oh that is Grandma Marion and Grandpa Sid," and that was so and so and on until the bride came marching down. Sue then said to me that she and Randy were embarrassed that they did not think to bring a gift, and I assured her that the envelope in my inside breast pocket was more than enough for all four of us, and that made her feel better.

Upon conclusion of the processional and the ceremony, we were all ushered into a rather large cocktail hour room and the hors d'oeurves began. First with lamb chops, and chicken being passed around and of course the traditional franks in a blanket, but then we all went over to the buffet and Sue and Randy almost fell over as they had never been to a lavish Jewish wedding and the food display bowled them over, but not enough to dissuade them from partaking mightily and rapidly.

At this point, Sue reiterated that she felt terrible that they did not bring a gift and I once again assured her that the envelope I had more than covered us all. Laura spied "Grandma Marion" and gave her a kiss and had the photographer snap their picture and then had all four of us pose with Grandma and the camera snapped away.

After about thirty minutes of indulgence, the lights began to flicker and we explained to them that dinner was about to be served. Sue said it was all so lovely that it was a shame that we could not stay and that was my opening to take "the envelope" out of my jacket pocket and ask her to open it so she would feel better about not having a gift with her.

She did just that and read.

Dear Sue and Randy,

As we were not invited to this wedding, but rather crashed it, and dinner is being served, and we do not belong here, it is time for us to get the (expletive) out of here, so let's go.

Sue looked at us and said "what is this, some kind of joke" and she handed the note to Randy who turned beet red and said NO you two are kidding us as for sure we belonged here as you seemed to know "everyone" and you two wouldn't do something like that."

We replied, "unless you want to get thrown out, let us get our asses out of here right now as we have successfully CRASHED THIS WEDDING and it is time to skedaddle."

With that Laura and I turned and started walking briskly out of the room and they, in total awe, followed and were additionally mortified as Laura grabbed one of the flower filled vases lining the staircase down to the main floor.

With them in tow, we exited the front of the Plaza and upon seeing us, Laura with the flowers, and Randy and Sue following with astonished looks on their respective faces, our driver Claude doubled over in laughter as he knew the deed has been perfectly accomplished. We entered the limo and Sue and Randy could still not believe what had just happened and they were both in shock that we would perpetrate such a "fraud" on the wedding people and on them in particular. As we drove down to our apartment on 37th st. they started to unwind and started to laugh their non Jewish tushies off in appreciation of what we had just pulled off.

What was truly astonishing is that the whole thing went off without a hitch. It could have been a scene from a Hollywood movie, but it was real life and our own sublime mystery night extravaganza. (And we did it years before "*THE WEDDING CRASHERS*" movie ever came out).

We arrived at our 37th st. apt and took our overnight bags upstairs and we all proceeded to change into our jeans and sweaters. When we descended, Claude and the limo, as pre arranged, were gone (as we did have some monetary constraints) and who was there to drive us, but Harry, the handyman that Sue and Randy had used a month earlier to take us down to Philadelphia.

Harry then took us to the theater where *STOMP* was playing and we settled into our mezzanine seats for a great performance.

When we exited, Harry, was there to take us downtown to Lucky Chans restaurant as we knew they both liked Chinese, but what they didn't know upon entering was that all the wait staff were men in drag and when that finally dawned on them, they again were in awe as they were certainly not familiar with this type of situation. They were really mid westerners at heart.

However after a few beers, we all settled in for the conclusion of our greatest mystery night ever. One the way home, we all agreed that would be the last as no one could think of anything that would top *THE WEDDING*.
What a night!!!!!

The postscript to the story!!!!

About two weeks after that Nov 17th evening, I was in my car driving home from the city and the phone rings (we used car phones back then) and it is Sue, and she is hysterical laughing and saying, "enough already Bernie," and that we are too much. I asked her what she was talking about and she said, "Stop the bull shit," I know you sent this thank you note. I said "what the hell are you talking about Sue?" and she just kept on going that yes it was funny, but "enough already."

I finally convinced her to read the thank you to me and it said.

Dear Sue and Randy,

Thank you so much for sharing our wedding evening with us and for your very generous gift. We have moved into our home just down the street from you in Brookville, and we would like to come over for coffee some night and get to know you better.

Sincerely,

Lisa and Nathan Nachman

I swore to her that I did not write the note and I knew nothing about it and that she needed to wait for me to get home to see if I received one too, and guess what? We did not!!!

A mystery indeed, especially since the note came on engraved stationery. ???

About a month later, Laura and I went to dinner with our friends, Beverly and Len Pace, she being a good friend of Laura's and Len was my physician.

Of course they knew about the wedding crashing, but we could not wait to relate the mystery of the "engraved thank you note."

Upon conclusion of our tale, both Len and Beverly had ear to ear grins and confessed to writing the note to punctuate just how easy it is to perpetrate a fraud.

Beverly had arranged to have the thank you note engraved and printed just to add some authenticity to their end of the hoax.

It was indeed a fitting conclusion to a most exciting adventure!!!!

BERNIE AND BUSES

As far back as my memory allows, when in a situation involving a lot of other people, I have always backed away from "following the crowd." When everyone seemed headed for the door on the right, I seem bent to heading in the opposite direction, not as an act of defiance, but strictly because my gut feeling usually pointed me in a different direction.

I offer that as my explanation for having an aversion to public buses as my mode of transportation. I like to be in control of my surroundings whenever possible, and since "I dance to a different drummer," traveling on a public bus does not offer me that option.

In the course of my business life, twice I deviated from this philosophy, and in both instances, bore the consequences of my decision; at least in my own mind.

On two separate occasions, when we found ourselves in Naples doing business over the Easter weekend, we flew off to Sicily for a long weekend as European commerce closed down for four days. On our first trip when we landed at Catania, we traveled by private car to the San Domenico Palace Hotel in Taormina which was about an hour and a half very pleasant drive away.

On our second trip, Laura thought it would be fun to take the local bus from the airport to Taormina so we could be "immersed in some of the local culture." We caught an 8 PM bus which was loaded with locals, carrying their marketing products which included live poultry some of which was "topside" in crates, strapped down to the roof. The bus stopped every fifteen minutes at the numerous rural stops along the way, with some people departing with their fish and live fowl, and some coming on board for the rest of the trip. After two hours of this, I was ready to "abandon" ship, but of course I demurred to my lovely wife and her desire to "be immersed." Finally about 10:45 we were the only remaining passengers and it was pitch dark as we pulled into Taormina and the bus proceeded thru some back streets that were not only dark, but also deserted.

The driver explained in Italian to Laura, that he was taking the bus to his house and he would then drive us in his car to the hotel. I remember turning to Laura and saying "we are going to be robbed and killed for sure." We then stopped in some unlit back alley and the driver got up and started walking down the aisle to us and I said, "This is it. We are done for." He reached overhead and took down our two suitcases and motioned to follow him which we reluctantly did. He then opened the doors to his car, and we got in as he put our suitcases in the trunk. Two minutes later, thankfully, we found ourselves in front of the San Domenico Palace Hotel where we had become a "late arrival." When we explained to the desk clerks why we were delayed, they all burst into laughter as they well knew the ride we had just endured, "immersed" in the local culture. Four days later, somewhat tanned and relaxed, you can rest assured that we took a car service back to the airport.

Our next business bus episode occurred about ten years later in Frankfurt Germany during our initial visit to the Frankfurt Fair.

Upon arrival and registering at the Frankfurt Kempinski Hotel, Laura noted a sign "courtesy bus service to the Fair" which of course she inquired about. It seemed that the hotel was offering gratis bus service directly from the hotel lobby to the Fair entrance. I then checked and was told the bus travels non stop from the hotel directly to the Fair. So we signed up for the 8AM jaunt the following morning.

We boarded on time right in front of the hotel and the driver confirmed he was going directly to the Fair, but minutes later, as he pulled away from the hotel, I noticed he took a left turn when I knew the Fair was definitely in the other direction. I thought maybe there was a back way so I kept quiet for a few minutes until I realized we were not making any kind of appropriate turn towards the Fair. When I got up and questioned the driver, he said he had received last minute instructions to pick up a Japanese contingent from one of the other hotels on the other side of town. After stopping to pick up that group, the bus was standing room only and it was now 8:30 and we were just getting en route to the Fair.

At 9 AM, the opening time for the Fair, we were still at least ½ mile away and I could see the entrance across a rather large green belt area, but we were now sitting in bumper to bumper traffic, and I finally bolted up and said "open the doors, we are getting out."

With Laura in tow we shoved our way thru the aisle and out the door. Everyone then gawked at us in disbelief as we trudged across the green lawn which took about ten minutes.

When we arrived at the entrance, I looked back and saw the bus in the very same spot we had left it, so I knew I had made the right decision.

We arrived at our booth and proceeded to set up, but of course when no one showed up for the first ½ hour, I had to endure those knowing glances of Ms. Laura who told me when I decided to bail out. "What are you carrying on about? You know no one will show up at the booth until 10." She too was right, as usual!!!!!!

Still, I was livid for not listening to myself and not taking a taxi as we usually did. To this day I have never again entered a public bus, nor will I.

Just my own hang up!!!!

FLORIDA, St. MARTIN, AND MIRABELLE

The Island of St. Martin played a significant role in our lives ever since our very first visit back in the late 70's when we vacationed at one of the rental apartments at Mullet Bay with all four of my daughters. We returned a couple of times and were seriously considering a purchase of a two bedroom unit at Mullet Bay, or with friends, a three bedroom unit at Cupecoy or even property on the top of Mount Rouge. Frankly, as it turned out then, I was not sophisticated enough to wrap my arms around the purchase of property outside of the States, which is why in 1979 we ended up at Sloan's Curve in Palm Beach.

Laura and I agreed that Miami, Hollywood, or Ft. Lauderdale were not for us, so I volunteered to visit the West Coast of Florida to see what the Tampa/St. Petersburg area was like. I loved Sarasota and Longboat key, but after a few days I determined that the West coast of Florida was not for us either. A few weeks later, Laura and I started our exploration of the East Coast starting with Key Biscayne and working our way up to Boca Raton and then eventually up to Palm Beach. Since my parents were living in Palm Beach, it was not our first choice, but as luck would have it, we "discovered" 2000 Ocean Blvd, Sloans Curve, a two building complex that was just being developed on Palm Beach Island, just ½ mile from where my folks were residing in the Harbor House. We fell in love with the layout of the apartment and its location with a lovely view of the Intercoastal waterway, and less then ten minutes from Worth Ave.

After submitting a down payment on a large two bedroom apartment, the developer, Sandy Weinstein, "twisted our arm" to buy one of the pool side cabanas. He knew from past experience they would be in great demand once the complex was sold out since there were twice as many apartments as cabanas. Under his urging we did in fact buy one, but refused to spend a lot of money decorating it as many others were doing. Laura came up with the unique idea of renting it. That is just what we did for two years, until the renter wanted to fix it up and offered to buy it for about three times what we paid for it. We sold it quickly!!!!! Sandy had told us that no one had ever thought about renting out a cabana, and he was delightfully surprised by our experience. Kudos to Ms. Laura.

We enjoyed ten years of vacations there (1979-89) and became charter members of the Falls Country Club, where I did get to play some golf. Eventually, as the girls got older they became bored with Palm Beach and wanted a livelier venue. In addition we were all fed up with coming down at Xmas and wearing sweaters instead of bathing suits. We opted to sell the apartment, and decided to re visit St. Martin, where every morning the sun came up like a ball of orange gold and warmed our hearts and bodies.

Our first few re- visits were to La Samanna, but once the girls started bringing friends, it became too pricey and we ventured out to the world of villa rentals, and that is how we eventually ended up building our Caribbean dream house.

We utilized the Carimo Real Estate Company for all our rentals as they represented about forty upscale houses on the French side. From 1990 to 1995, vacationing with our girls, and on numerous occasions with friends, we must have stayed in at least fifteen villas. Every time Laura liked a house, it was designed by a French archi-tect named Joel, who worked closely with the Carimo group to design villas that were properly laid out for rental purposes. (all bedrooms of equal size).

After three of years of renting, we decided it was time to buy a piece of land and build our Caribbean dream house, and so it was that every time we visited the Island, Francis, the owner of Carimo, would take us around to available home sites. It took him two years to finally find "the spot." I remember him calling us and say-ing he received a listing for a large water front parcel on Simpsons Bay that he thought would be perfect for what we wanted, as we had specified water front, fab-ulous view, and a great degree of privacy.

It was with some excited trepidation that we met him and walked through the underbrush of this six acre water front site to eventually exit at the waters edge where we stopped in our tracks, looked at each other, and I said "oh my god, we are in trouble." He had just that morning received the listing from a lady who was being awarded the parcel as her divorce settlement and she was interested in selling the whole parcel, rather than incurring the expense and time of splitting it into two saleable lots.

The parcel was at the "wrong" end of Simpsons Bay, in an undeveloped area with an open field on the left and a dilapidated "drug house" on the right. That gave us pause to think. Did we really want to "pioneer" this part of the lagoon? We decided to "bite the bullet," buy the entire six acre site, split it in half and sell off the lower lot and keep the raised bluff parcel for the building of our home. Well, it took over four years to sell the lower acreage, which is why we did not break ground for our home until February 2000. We were going to use the proceeds of the sale to help with the financing of building our home, which is exactly what we eventually ended up doing.

In the intervening years, we met on different occasions with Joel and his daughter Julie and we described exactly how we wanted our Caribbean home to turn out since we knew precisely what we liked and disliked in the many Joel designed homes that we had stayed in. We knew we wanted a great deal of outside space, both covered and uncovered, as we realized that on each vacation, we ended up spending most of our leisure time in "outside space" as opposed to closed in space. Consequently, 60 % of our home was "open" and afforded us and our eventual renters, unfettered access to the elements of sun, water and cool sea breezes that came across the bay almost daily. In addition, I insisted on an oversized pool so I could easily swim laps as that was my tropical exercise of choice.

As we made no changes in the original plans, Joel was able to have the house completed in less than ten months; an unbelievable feat for Island construction. This, he accomplished in spite of the fact that his legal situation precluded him from visiting the French side of the Island during the entire construction process. It seems, he had been found guilty of employing "illegal's" in one of his prior building projects and was banned from entering the French side of the Island until well after our construction was finished. He had his son in law, Laurent, in charge of construction, but he did sneak a peak on Saturdays, when he had permission to visit his doctors, so we knew he had his eye on the job at all times.

As promised, the house was habitable by Thanksgiving of 2000 just ten months after ground was broken, and the house was 100% completed in time for the Xmas rental in December.

We had a delightful experience in building our home, and all of this was accomplished without us making visits to the island as each week we received progress pictures via the internet. We had complete confidence in Joel's ability and integrity, and our confidence was amply rewarded.

When we first signed the contract to build, Laura started "furnishing the house" up here in the States. We leased a forty foot storage container and placed it at the end of our long driveway and just about every weekend, we were at the ABC carpet outlet store or involved in the re finishing and re upholstering of some of the furniture we had kept from our Florida apartment. At any rate, having a set of plans from which we did not deviate, enabled Laura to furnish Mirabelle, before it was completed. When we were finished, and the container was full, we dispatched it to St. Martin and arranged to be there when it arrived. Within twenty four hours the house was completely furnished, and the pictures hung, and everyone that was associated with the building of the house i.e.: the landscapers, the stone man, and Joel's family, were in awe that the house "was done" and totally habitable and rentable.

They all had done their job and we had done ours.

I then commissioned a boat dock and built a set of stairs leading down to our care-taker's cottage and the water. Shortly thereafter, I purchased a 24 ft Whaler from a friend of ours that was buying a larger boat, so three months after taking possession, I had my own boat docked right below the bluff, and that was a life long dream come true for me.

In the interim, the "drug house" next door had been purchased at foreclosure by a lovely Belgian couple who did a total renovation and cleaned up and landscaped the property and occupied it as their primary residence. Additionally, on the par-cel we had sold, now stood a lovely five bedroom home. Both houses soon "sported" a boat dock too, and miraculously that end of the bay. became "the hot spot."

We ended up using the Whaler for five years and then selling it so I could purchase a custom fitted 20 ft Apex inflatable which was just perfect for use in the bay and along the coast line, and we really enjoyed the pleasure and convenience of having our boat docked at the house.

We had designed Mirabelle as a rental house. Maintaining an Island home was a costly affair and fortunately during our first seven years at Mirabelle, the rental income more than offset our maintenance costs, and in the beginning also covered a portion of our mortgage expenses.

Even when the Euro was first introduced we were doing quite well in covering our costs, but in 2007 the American dollar started to lose value against the Euro. Since our income was strictly in dollars and 95% of our costs were in Euros, the rental income started to erode, and we had to constantly "reach into our pocket" to cover the expenses, which was certainly not our original plan for the property.

The growing expense vs. income disparity prompted us to put the house up for sale and move on to a more economically friendly location. We purchased a lovely panoramic mountain side site on the Pacific Coast of Costa Rica, and we ended up selling Mirabelle in January of 2010, after ten great years.

Unfortunately, Laura passed away six weeks later, so I abandoned any Costa Rica building plans. I still own the land and hopefully when the global economy improves, I will be able to sell it, as I would never consider building another Island home without Laura by my side.

The whole Island experience was a positive one and we know we were responsible for our new friends, Charles and Ardith, purchasing a home, renovating it with Joel, and enjoying it to this very day.

We were very lucky to have "discovered" Joel and his daughter and son in law as they made the entire construction process very smooth and stress free.

I had fulfilled my life time dream of owning a home in the Caribbean, with my own boat dock and small boat.   In the end, not only did we have a great ten year run, but made a handsome profit when selling.

CHAMPAGNE COUNTRY WITH RANDY AND SUE

Laura and I were scheduled to attend the Premier Class show in Paris in September of '88 when Sue and Randy said they would love to join us there for a mini vacation. They had never been to Paris, and thought it would be fun to be there with us.

I explained that we would be working over the weekend but that we would certainly point them in the right direction for interesting sight seeing during the day, and we would hook up with them for dinners. We also agreed to stay on a few days after the show to spend time with them, and to visit the Champagne country in Reims outside of Paris where we had never ventured.

So we rented a car on the Tuesday after the show and Randy drove us out to the country and into Reims with me as the navigator. Everyone who knows me is aware that I possess an excellent sense of direction (except after smoking) and have good map reading skills to boot, so we did not anticipate any difficulties.

After about an hour we found ourselves in the most beautiful country side filled with vineyards as far as the eye could see.

Our first stop was the Taittinger cellars where we took the traditional tour and sipped a little of the bubbly on our way out as we were heading to the very famous Les Crayeres Chateau and Restaurant in Reims itself. Upon leaving Taittinger, I received detailed verbal directions to Les Crayeres, but after about fifteen minutes of wandering, I admitted we were hopelessly lost. Anyone I approached did not speak English so we were pretty helpless. I finally spied a taxi and told Randy to pull up behind it so I could hopefully get directions to the restaurant. The driver did not seem to know where Blvd. Henry Vasner was and it was not until I mentioned Les Crayeres that his eyes lit up and he said. Oui, monsieur Les Crayeres!!! And he started to give me directions in French. I said, one moment sir and went back to the car and told Randy to just follow me. The three of them, Laura, Sue and Randy, all gave me a blank stare and asked me where the hell I was going?
I reiterated, "Just follow me."

I then jumped in to the taxi and said, "Monsieur, Les Crayeres sil vous plait," and five minutes later after a lot of twists and turns, both the taxi and our rental car entered a ten acre "park" discreetly nestled among lush gardens off of Blvd. Henry Vasner, which I never would have been able to find on my own. For a cab fare of about U.S. $ 10 we averted a potential disaster and I averted any further personal embarrassment.

We all had a good laugh about that and then entered a most elegant and sophisticated chateau that took our collective breathes away.

Upon entering the dining room, I must say, although nicely attired, I felt underdressed for one of the few times in my life, as we surely were seated in the midst of what must have been the nattily attired Parisian "upper crust" and other well groomed Europeans, who normally "lunched" like this on a Tuesday in the country.

When we viewed the menu, Laura, Randy and I were all ready to leave as we knew we were in for a $ 400 plus luncheon before ordering any bubbly. Sue insisted we stay, as this was going to be a once in a lifetime experience for her.

Now none of us in the foursome was anywhere near a gourmet, especially since you already know that Randy's choice of upscale dining was spaghetti and meat balls and his drink of choice was a diet Pepsi. However, I must say we all immensely enjoyed some of the finest food I had ever tasted, accompanied, as you might imagine, by some outstanding champagne. Ask me not what we dined on, but I just remember it being very special from start to finish.

It was a day to remember which we have often referenced on many occasions, especially everyone's fond memories of my navigational break down and creative recovery.

HAVING A WEDDING AT HOME IS NOT A PARTY

Unless of course, money is no object

If you can afford a wedding planner, a wedding coordinator and a wedding day supervisor to create, supervise and stage your at home wedding, then this tale is not for you.

If your funds are plentiful and spending on an affair at home is no problem, including the home improvements that will be required once you start, then your home wedding can be a party for you, the bride and groom, and your guests.

However, if you are like most people, you need to proceed with a budget in mind, which for us negated hiring all the professionals who could have made our life easy, but hiring the "right" people to coordinate the affair would have far exceeded the resources we allotted to a garden wedding.

The bride and groom had previously agreed it would be more important for us to help them with the down payment on a home rather than finance an extravagant affair, and on that we heartily concurred.

Undaunted by the project, Laura and I knew, or so we thought, that our combined organizational skills, and her experience in the food industry, would allow us to sail through this party as we had done so often in the past. Never did we realize that all my logistical and her culinary and party preparation "expertise" would soon be stretched to the limits and beyond.

So let us now back peddle a little to give you some historical set up information.

As previously indicated, in late 1972, 1 ½ years after our marriage, we started house looking and in February of 1973 "discovered" Ambience, a 3+acre park like setting located in Muttontown, within reasonable commuting distance from mid-town New York.

Our friends referred to it as Shapiro Park and even gifted us cocktail napkins that read just that. I remember sitting on the hillside, looking down on the house and the major part of the property with my friend, Morty Gropper, who had three young boys, and all he could talk about was having their Bar Mitzvahs right there on the back lawn.

In those early years, the lawn area was quite a bit smaller, as we also had the original estate green house and cold bins which took up about an acre. At that time the green house was in good repair and being tended by a professional gardener and Laura was cutting daily.

We finally demolished the green house in the mid 1990's when it became extremely difficult to find workers to maintain this wonderful glass structure, and the price of oil made home grown flowers economically unfeasible. So we ended up with another acre of lawn, which eventually was to be the exact spot that housed our wedding tent (but that is really jumping ahead in the story).

Most of our friends continued to reside in Roslyn or thereabouts and mostly on 1/3 acre home sites, so our situation appeared quite large in their eyes and they often talked about us renting the premises out for weddings, Bar Mitzvahs, sweet sixteen's, all of which of course were out of the question as far as we were concerned. (Well maybe Laura would have agreed, but we never really had any serious conversation about the concept in those early years). I did know however, Laura fantasized that maybe some day we would have our own daughter's wedding on the lawn.

Almost immediately after purchasing the house, we discussed installing a pool on the premises and most of the conventional wisdom (my father, her father, and the pool professionals) all agreed that it would be most convenient to place the pool in the lawn area near the house.

However, Laura correctly determined that she really did not want to see the pool all winter from the living room, or any of the bedrooms, as a pool in winter is not really a pretty sight, as you are essentially looking at a mesh cover secured to a patio. She finally convinced everyone that the pool should be on the hilltop at the rear of our property.

She declared that any inconvenience caused by the long distance from the house, could be overcome by building a full service pool house, with a kitchenette and changing rooms, so that once on the hill there would be no need to come down to the house during the day.

We did just that during the 1974/75 season and she was correct: once we and our guests went up to the pool, we stayed there for the entire day, concluding with a BBQ at the blue stone table we had constructed for just that purpose. We usually had anywhere from twelve to twenty friends (including their children) and the pool received full use for the next twenty years. I would joke in later years, that we definitely amortized the cost of the pool over that time span.

It was during this period (1973-1975) that Blair and Brie were born, and they were quickly initiated to the pool summer life style as we seldom left the property since our friends came every weekend with their children to enjoy "the country." During those fun filled days, the conversation would always turn to the site and how perfect it would be for a large celebration.

Both Blair and Brie having been born and raised at the house, also enjoyed the park like setting and experienced numerous swim parties, graduation parties and sweet sixteen parties at the pool, and of course they were at home for our winter Xmas parties, so they both knew what Laura was capable of doing at the house in the way of celebrations.

We finally decided to demolish the green house in the early 1990's due to disrepair and the high cost of maintenance and fuel. When we finally removed the structure and the three dozen twenty five foot arborvitaes screening it from the house, we were amazed at how the back lawn just "opened up" and really gave us a rather large expanse. Now you could see the beauty of the rock wall that ran all the way from the start of the rock garden to the far easterly end of the property.

As much as we had loved the flowers from the green house, we now realized how much of the property had been "hidden" by its presence. We loved the new open look and Laura then became very involved in cultivating the rock garden which now was in full view from the rear patio. I would venture to guess that it was this opening up of the property that really enforced Laura's desire to have a wedding at home.

The reality of a pending wedding materialized, when Brie and Todd decided after twelve years of dating, that it was time to reside together. They rented a cute one bedroom house in Glen Head in February of 2003, and officially became engaged at our annual Xmas party in mid-December of that year.

Prior to that, in November of 2003 they began looking at houses in the Glen Head area. I say looking because the concept of home ownership was not exactly a reality at that point, but fatefully they "discovered" a "move in" located directly on the 2nd hole of the Glen Head County Club. When Brie walked in, she said "this is my house," and since that is not something that happens very often, everyone agreed that this was an opportunity that should not be passed up. Having a home with two hundred and forty ft. directly on a golf course and next to the 2nd green is not an every day possibility, especially in this area.

Now the question arose as to whether it was more important to Brie and Todd to start off with a house or have a grand wedding celebration. They decided that for the long term, help with the down payment on the house far outweighed the short term allure of a large celebration. Kudos to them.

Brie expressed a desire to be married at home which of course thrilled Laura who had been dreaming of a garden wedding for many years, but now it was not to be a grand celebration with music and all the hoopla, but rather, an understated brunch, without live music and a dance floor, but just an "at home luncheon."

Deciding to have a wedding at home was not a frightening prospect for us as we had entertained twenty to seventy friends at numerous dinner and holiday parties so a wedding, we thought, would just be another party, and that was a major miscalculation on our part.

Our first order of business was to create the guest list, which miraculously grew from seventy five to a hundred and forty within a week. We had the Kraska guest list and Brie and Todd's list as well, and now the total was double the amount of people that we had ever previously entertained at home.

The second order of business was to select a date. Brie and Todd preferred the end of August, but Laura and Martha Kraska, Todd's mom, convinced them that the garden and grounds would be at their best at the beginning of August, as the end of the month would signal the end of the blooming season.

So what started out to be an August 22nd (the bride and groom's lucky #) became first August 14th and finally August 7th. It sounds so easy as I write, but believe me, date selection was a struggle (as most wedding details turned out to be). All the clichés about the stress created when planning a wedding are correct. Laura and I were used to making our decisions quickly and decisively, but now we had others to consider.

Once we established that August 7th was a good date for Brie and Todd's friends, our next order of business was to call Mc Brides Tent Company that had been recommended to us by our friend Sandy Gilder, who was formerly in the party planning business.

We had no idea how large a tent would be needed for our one hundred and twenty five guests as we were anticipating standard 10% fallout. Mc Brides advised us that if we were serving the buffet in the tent, but without a dance floor, that a 40' x 60' tent would be ample for a group of twelve tables. However, Laura toyed with the idea of setting up the buffet in the living room which she was prepared to "clean out" so that we could offer some air conditioned relief to our guests and the food as well, as we anticipated a typical hot and humid August day. We went back and forth on that decision for a while, but finally decided on the 40' x 60' out on the lawn, with the buffet stations located around the perimeter of the tent. Unfortunately, we could not place it as close to the house as we would have liked, as that was our "low ground" and we could not take a chance that it would be entirely dry for the party.

It was agreed that the tent should be placed on the high ground, which was exactly the location of the green house that had been demolished some seven years prior. At this very first meeting with the tent people, I was cautioned to mark out the sprinkler lines before the men drove the tent spikes into the grass. (Just another of the many details to be considered when planning that home garden party).

Of course, we wished for the best of weather conditions, but cautiously prepared for the worst by arranging for an additional smaller tent over our rear patio with two marquees on either side for bar stations. If weather dictated, we would have to squeeze everyone under this tent for the ceremony. Now, how about getting to the main tent from the patio in the case of rain? Well the solution that was offered to us by the representative (obviously they deal with these situations all the time) was to reserve a seventy five ft. marquee running from the patio tent to the main tent. All we had to do two days prior to the tent set up, was to decide if we wanted to install the marquee or just skip it and pay the reservation fee of 1/3 of the cost of the marquee, which is what we eventually did.

We had made our first step in coordinating the affair and it was only March, and plenty of time for all the other details, or so we thought. It was then that we started looking around at the property, which until recently looked fairly well maintained, but now we ventured back up to the pool and pool house and quickly realized that something would have to be done to spruce up this area. Unquestionably, if the weather was nice, many of Brie and Todd's friends would end up here at the pool in the late afternoon and early evening.

All we really needed to do was replace almost our entire three tiered brick coping that had deteriorated over the years (about 2000 bricks), re plumb the pool that had ceased to function about three years ago, and re marble dust the interior which was in poor shape from repeated acid washings. When the quotes arrived for this work, we rationalized that it could not be included into the wedding budget, as they were really capital improvements that would increase the value of the property in the coming years. The prospect was daunting, and we moved on to other considerations before making any final decisions.

We talked about painting the house, re doing the driveway that needed more gravel and other "minor" household repairs, but again the quotes were high enough to prompt us to put off any final decisions on home improvements. Were we sticking our heads temporarily in the sand? Yes of course we were. We both finally realized that all of this work would have to be accomplished if we were to have the wedding in the garden.

We then started to visit caterers which became arduous for Laura as she was quite experienced in preparing large quantities of food. She was tempted to call our friend and exquisite chef, Roy Daniels up from Florida, and supervise the catering herself. Roy would have prepared a superior menu, but he no longer had a service team up North and that was the one advantage the local caterers offered. Everyone finally convinced her (which she really already knew) that doing the catering herself for a wedding, would create undue pressure and she would not then be a guest at what we still were calling "a party."

Based on family relationships, recommendations and advertisements in local wedding magazines, we visited four local upscale caterers, none of whom seemed to understand Laura's concept of "a casual home brunch wedding." They all came back with very fancy menus and prices to match, and Laura was becoming quite frustrated. She was almost ready to call Roy, and take her chances with staffing when our friend Ardith recommended a caterer from Island Park that had catered a number of events that she had attended.

Her message was, "the food was good, but the presentation left something to be desired." At any rate, Laura visited with this caterer and returned feeling that here was a real commissary that seemed to grasp her concept of a simple brunch without a lot of fanfare.

Their price was similar to all the other caterers, but it included the staff (a big deal when you are dealing with 14 service people). So a caterer had been selected. He visited the house in early May and a tentative menu was discussed and agreed upon, but Laura bristled at the thought of renting commercial glasses, plates, flatware and linens.

She knew that these were items when set on the table would establish the mood for the affair and she insisted on selecting them herself. Translated, that means she spent a great deal of time, energy, and gas, **finding and buying** what was to be on the table, at the buffet stations, and on the bars.

The caterer told her she would regret this decision as we needed over five hundred glasses (champagne, wine and water) over four hundred plates (soup, lunch, and dessert) and of course one hundred and fifty + sets of flatware (five pcs. to a set = seven hundred and fifty pcs.), but buy them she did and regrets were non existent. After that, we did not see or speak to the caterer until ten days before the wedding when Laura finalized the menu.

Now you must try to understand that the middle of May is approaching and we are due to visit Provence, France with our friends Randy and Sue Jones (our wedding crashing friends) for our end of a house swap deal for our St. Martin vacation home (from May 14th to 25th). Off we went with about a thousand details yet to be addressed. What me worry? No, Laura was used to "pulling" everything together at the last minute. Undaunted, we had a super house swapping vacation experience with our friends and returned on the 25th and swung into action.

Brie wanted orange and pink as her color theme and Laura was nervous about finding appropriate flowers to plant at the house to coordinate with those colors. Planting became a first priority as Laura wanted to be sure that all was in major bloom during the first ten days of August. So, in the midst of all else, daily trips to the nurseries became de rigor and the jeep started to resemble a pick up truck, dirt and all. Of course when Laura ordered a hundred and fifty flats of impatiens, those were delivered directly to the court yard. That was quite a sight, and during the next four weeks, Laura's routine was to get up at the crack of dawn and plant as much as she could before the heat of the day overcame her and the plants. Pink and orange flowers were available and abundantly planted and the guests at the wedding certainly noted them. Of course she employed some help as the task of planting this property with a plethora of flowers is more than one can handle, especially since that was only one of the tasks to be tackled.

Now that we had a color theme, the invitations were next on the list. Working backwards for a July 10th response, they needed to be mailed by the first week in June in order to meet the six week etiquette rule. The quest for invitations was complicated by the fact that nothing we saw seemed to be appropriate for an informal garden brunch wedding.

Finally with the help of a friend, who is in the business, Laura created an invitation that really captured the mood of a lawn wedding with a touch of pink and orange to blend with the colors of the day. It was not formal and kind of light hearted, which is the mood that we wanted to convey. Neither dress nor driving instructions were included as almost every guest had been to our home for a dinner or Xmas celebration and we relied upon everyone to dress "appropriately."

With the invitations ordered, Laura turned her thoughts to the linens to be used on the tables under the tent. It took a while but she finally found a floral tablecloth that "shouted" garden party and appropriate buffet table coverings as well. As to the napkins, Laura really didn't like what was available for rental, so she ended up buying one hundred and fifty napkins that she liked. Are you now getting the message that perhaps she was planning on opening a catering business after the wedding? Not so……. although we have had requests from friends over the years.

The table was set or so it seemed, but now Laura needed the finishing touch of a "charger" plate. If you have ever been to our home for dinner, you always had a charger plate greet you before the meal as it adds a touch of elegance to any table setting.

However, since we were in the orange/pink mode, finding the appropriate charger plate became a chore. Yes, Laura could go have gone to Saks or Bloomies and paid $ 25 each and bought a hundred and twenty five orange chargers, but the challenge came in finding them at a somewhat affordable price. Laura went so far as to be in touch with a manufacturer in Germany, who would ship them to us at the wholesale price, but after the duty, handling and shipping, they would also be quite expensive. Her quest led to numerous phone calls, and she did manage to corral eighty five of them at a decent price. The other forty? Well, you could buy plain gold or silver chargers reasonably and spray paint them, but that experiment did not do well. Finally, a week before the wedding, Brie spray painted glass chargers on the back side only, but of course when on the table, they looked the same as all the others, especially since they spent hours matching the color of the "real" orange chargers. It was a major project, but they certainly added a touch of elegance to the table on the wedding day.

The invitations arrived and were perfect, and we now proceed to assemble the correct names and addresses of all the invitees and off to the calligrapher they went.

Now it was my task to handle the music, which was not an overwhelming assignment, since we had decided on no dancing at this early afternoon affair. After I spent hours on the internet investigating appropriate groups, Brie received a recommendation from a fellow teacher about three sisters (The Kende trio) from Locust Valley that were accomplished Julliard/Princeton University, musicians. I contacted their mom, Lisa who sent us a DVD of the girls and their music, and invited us to a concert at Old Westbury Gardens in mid June. We loved their looks and their music and hoped they could play at the ceremony and cocktail hour. Luck was on our side as they were touring Italy in July and would return on the 29th in plenty of time to play at the wedding. This was probably the easiest assignment on the wedding task list, and of course I chose to make that my responsibility. We spoke the night before the wedding to pre select a few songs, but basically, the girls played their normal wedding selections and they were charming and just right for the mood we wished to convey. My other assignment was the valet parking (I had all the easy stuff), and a call to Richie of Executive Parking was all that was needed. (Or was it?).

Now I ask you to remember that we had a "to do" list for the exterior of the house and property which we had not yet addressed. Lo and behold, Jose and his helper Alex appear at our door step because Jose was no longer employed by our landscape company and he wanted to know if we had any masonry work for him. Laura had discussed this with him weeks before, but we doubted if he would ever show up. I inquired if he could fix our rear patio as it was quite uneven from years of settling and the roots of the honey locust trees had raised the blue stone in many areas. He said NO PROBLEM and I reluctantly agreed to let him show us what he could do as this was the first week in June...

Jose asked me to buy some fine sand and he would lift all the blue stone, cut out the protruding roots, level the ground, pack it with the new fine sand and re-lay the old bluestone as we wanted to keep the look of the old rather than buy new stone. This was an aesthetic decision, not a financial one

This was my first step in becoming the general contractor for all the outside work at the house. Little did I know what awaited me for the next eight weeks.

Not wanting to "dump" sand and mess up the court yard, I made numerous trips to the masonry yard to buy bagged sand, which was both heavy to lift and more expensive to buy then if I had two or three yards delivered. Jose started to lift the stone, numbering each piece so I could be sure he would re-lay the patio as it was. I was doubtful, but a week later, we had a level patio that looked old, but newly done and I was amazed and really pleasantly surprised.

I asked him about the brick steps leading up to the pool and he replied, "NO PROBLEM, just buy some cement and cement sand" (which I learned is different from the fine sand used to level the blue stone patio). I did, and three days later the steps were repaired, using old brick that we had on the property. Again, I was amazed and very pleasantly surprised by his ability to do the job, so I sheepishly asked him to look at the pool and the four planters around and in the pool. His reply was "NO PROBLEM; just buy the brick and the cement and the trowels etc." Well now I had to match the old brick as Nassau Brick Co. was no longer in business and since we were repairing not replacing all the brick, we needed a match.

I called upon my neighbor on Remsens Lane, who is in the brick/stone construction business and he graciously came over and offered his advice and help. Mike had quoted on the job two years prior and it was quite expensive. I needed him to tell me if Jose and Alex could really do this job in the time frame required. He looked at the patio and brick steps and agreed that they could do the job, and since I was to be the general contractor, it would be somewhat reasonable.

Again, I was nervous and doubtful as I knew once we started on demolishing and removing the old brick, we would immediately pass the point of no return, so I asked Jose to first show me what he could do by repairing one of the four brick planters that were placed within the pool. He attacked it the first morning and one entire wall collapsed and I thought the "game was over."

He proceeded to take down the rest of the planter, while Mike took me to his favorite local masonry supply yard. There we found a close match to the old brick and I promptly ordered five hundred, which was a palette full and more than I anticipated needing. The next morning, the bricks, cinder blocks (to shore up the brick planters that we were to redo), two yards of cement sand and countless Portland cement bags were dropped in the court yard (the same court yard I did not want to mess up when doing the patio, but now it was serious construction going on at the house). Jose and Alex then proceeded to wheelbarrow all the building materials up to the pool area, which was a job in itself as I would not allow a machine to traverse the lawn.

By the following evening, Jose had rebuilt 80% of the collapsed planter and he had done an excellent job, and I felt better about doing this project that all the professionals had warned me would be a major undertaking (we eventually replaced fourteen hundred bricks).

When the planter was finished we walked around the pool and decided which bricks to replace and which to leave and the following day they started to "jack hammer" out the old bricks using hand chisels and sledge hammers. Needless to say it was messy and a lot of construction debris was ending up in the pool itself, but Jose assured me he would clean it all up when the brick work was completed. NO PROBLEM.

Two days into the job, Haven pools showed up to start to rip up the blue stone patio in an effort to reach our "sunken" skimmer lines (a great look, but not practical for repair work). Little did I know in 1974, that one day the plumbing would have to be replaced.

The bad news was that the patio had to be ripped up and the cement chiseled out to a six foot depth to reach the return lines. The good news was that Haven pools, the builder of the pool in 1974 was still in business, and the son Craig was running the company. The bad news was, my thirty year warranty had expired (a sick joke), but the good news was, Craig said that he could get the pool to work just fine by replacing only one of the skimmer lines and installing two new return lines, rather than dig up the entire(rather large) patio to reach all four skimmers. The pool area soon resembled a war zone and I wondered if it would all be put back together again in time for the wedding.

Please remember, after all this work, the inside of the pool still had to be refinished. A friend and neighbor suggested we paint the interior of the pool rather than incur the large expense of marble dusting. I was dubious, but after researching the procedure and learning that the right paints was available from Leslie's pool supply at a very competitive price, the decision was easy as long as we had someone to paint it. Fortuitously, our "painter," Gregg had just finished a job and was now available to start on the house and he agreed to do the pool when the construction was finished. Four weeks later, early in July, it appeared that the brick and plumbing work at the pool would be completed around July 10th and the painting could proceed.

The problem with painting a pool is that you need the interior surface to be completely dry for a few days, & you need at least three dry days to paint the pool and then another three for the paint to dry. So the logistics were obvious: we needed about nine to ten days of consecutive dry weather, starting on or around July 10th. Well, we never did get exactly what we needed, but Mother Nature cooperated enough so that Gregg could actually finish the second coat on July 20th, and three days later I started filling the pool, which itself is a four day procedure (63,000 gallons). It was on July 27th that Haven could finally return to start up the filter system & not until the 30th when the pool was working well. (Kind of close to the wedding date, don't you think?)

It was at this point that I started to confide to my close friends that

HAVING A WEDDING AT HOME...... IS NOT A PARTY

Jose and Alex had finished at the pool and now I was a believer, so we asked them if they could install Belgian block for the six hundred linear feet of our driveway that sorely needed a cosmetic uplift. He said, NO PROBLEM. They then proceeded to trench the entire outline of our driveway and had cement and sand delivered to the court yard I had tried so hard to protect.

This now was another three week project that was going on while the pool was being plumbed and painted. Concurrently, the tree company that we hired showed up on schedule, with five men, and spent four hours pruning around the perimeter of the house. At the same time our very talented handyman, John took me to home depot where we purchased the necessary lumber for him to duplicate the front gate to our courtyard entrance, as it was over 40 years old & in disrepair...

HAVING A WEDDING AT HOME... IS NOT A PARTY...
BECAME MY DAILY MANTRA

The replies started to arrive and it became obvious that our anticipated count of one hundred and twenty five guests would prove to be very accurate, so twelve tables were appropriate and we were on track. We were up at 5:30 AM every morning, planting, ordering construction materials and coordinating all the vendors that were involved. I then went to work at 9:30 at the Muttontown Village Hall and would get back to wedding business around 1PM, by which time Laura had planted, returned from purchasing all the many items she needed for the "party" and we then started again on outside activity.

An important item that had to be settled was the wedding cake. Brie had found an "offbeat" cake that she loved, but it came from an Oregon baker and was frightfully expensive and the thought of shipping the cake cross country was not really viable. Brie suggested the French bakery in our area and we all visited with Danielle, the Italian owner of Le Bonne Boulangerie, in East Norwich, and as it turned out he was Blair's classmate at B.U. back in the early 90's. When he was shown the picture, he immediately gravitated to it and said......... NO PROBLEM!!!!

Donnie wisely suggested that we only order a cake for seventy five people to keep the expense down, and he would prepare a sheet cake for the full guest list with the exact raspberry filling of the cake itself. We agreed and the cake was ordered on June 18th.

Laura and Brie then began the quest for a photographer that they were comfortable with as Brie really did not want a lot of traditional posed pictures, but rather more candid shots, and mostly in black and white. After many hours on the internet, they contacted a local photographer in Huntington that appealed to both of them. They visited with her and finalized the arrangement on June 22nd, with Pam's commitment that she would show up on Friday, August 6th, to take some "getting ready" shots and familiarize herself with the grounds and pinpoint her best photographic locations.

My dear friend Paul arrived from his bucolic homestead at the Boulders in Scottsdale on July 13th for his annual summer vacation (he has been coming here in July for many years in an effort to escape the Phoenix summers) and he anticipated helping, but little did he know he was coming to a full working ranch for his month long stay. I am not sure what we would have done without his help in running multiple errands every day. I am sure that he left on August 13th in shock and sorely needing his upcoming Canadian vacation.

Brie and Laura agreed that the flowers were very important, but since the garden was so abundantly planted, they agreed the table arrangements should be simple & natural looking and that each was to be placed in one of Laura's own treasured cut crystal bowls(some of which belonged to Laura's mom).

Merriel of Weston Floral Design, a very creative floral arranger that our daughter Blair had "discovered" as part of her party planning experiences, visited and discussed all of the flowers, both in and out of the house, and the garland to be used on the wedding arch. After this initial meeting, all other discussions were over the phone. Laura had seen much of Merriel's work, and had recommended her to a number of our friends and all were quite pleased, so Laura was confident that Merriel would capture the mood of the day in her floral creations.

On July 15th we had a dinner at the house, bringing together, Brie and Todd, his parents, Martha and Peter, Paul, ourselves, and the Mayor of Muttontown, Richard Murcott, and his wife Mary. The Mayor had agreed to officiate at the wedding and we felt it important that all the "players" should meet and have some discussion about the wedding. The basic details of the ceremony were discussed and agreed upon and that was one of the easiest parts of the preparation with nothing much else to do until the Mayor decided two days later that perhaps it would be best to have an amplification system for the ceremony so that everyone could hear. Having the Mayor officiate really made this a Muttontown affair, and it was a real nice touch to what we hoped would come across as a genuine home wedding.

We agreed and gave the assignment of a sound amplification to Paul, who promptly lined up a local company that would rent us a system for the weekend. This we decided could also be used for the background music we wished to play during the brunch. We concluded that rental on July 21st, and basically that was the last of the ten major vendors that we had to deal with. So basically, three weeks before the event, most of the major items had been arranged for.

We now had to deal with the wine, champagne and soft drinks. Fortunately, the Mayors brother in law owned the Osprey Vineyards in Southold and we were able to order all of our alcoholic needs directly from the Vineyard. We also purchased gin and vodka, but since this was a brunch we did not anticipate an abundance of hard liquor being consumed. We also ordered a special Paulaner Heiffen Weisen Munich beer at the behest of Brie, Todd and Peter Kraska. As a special treat we also ordered a few cases of Lindeman's Framboise beer from Belgium; red in color, and almost champagne in texture, and it proved to be a big hit with everyone that tasted it. We also arranged for all of the soft drinks and water, which Laura wanted poured exclusively from her cut glass pitchers.

One week prior to the wedding we finalized the menu with the caterer and coordinated all of the rental items with one of the recommended Long Island rental companies. I then touched base with all ten of the vendors, confirming the orders and delivery schedule.

We realized at this point that we needed additional storage space as Laura wanted to create twelve large boxes, with the service for each table, so that when the caterers arrived they would find each box labeled by table #, and containing all the elements necessary for setting the mood. Once this was done, we needed outside storage, so we purchased a shed and had it assembled behind the tree line and adjacent to where the cook's tent was to be set up. This also gave us an area for all the liquor and soft drinks and was definitely a necessity.

The week before the wedding was filled with last minute details; obtaining fabric for the bridal party walkway, tailoring of clothes, finalizing potted plantings around the house, the installation of dedicated electric lines to the cook's tent area, checking on all the circuit breakers, etc.

Martha and Peter arrived on the Sunday prior to the wedding to help Laura with the floral installation of the pool planters and to deliver plywood for a floor for our new storage shed. Gregg was finishing up painting the trim on the house and he called upon his friend to set up a scaffold so he could paint the two cupolas as well. When we realized this, I quickly went on line and located a crowing rooster weather vane (ours had blown down 15 years earlier) in stock at a source in New Hyde Park, and I picked it up the following morning and by days end it was installed.

I felt that we needed to make additional parking arrangements as it would be impossible to park sixty cars on Remsens Lane, so on Monday we mailed special parking instructions to half of our guests asking them to park at the Old Brookville Church. I then arranged for a van to shuttle our guests from the Church to the house, with one of our valets available for the return trip.

Everyone we ran into asked if we were ready for the party and my answer was always the same, and I think Laura, Brie, Blair & Paul all now concurred when I replied;

YES .... BUT

HAVING A WEDDING AT HOME   IS NOT A PARTY.

As Saturday approached, we worked on the remaining chores on our list (this was about the tenth time we updated the list) of things to do during the final days prior to the wedding, and some were assigned to Paul, some to Brie, and some to me, and all the rest to Laura.

On Monday, the cesspool people arrived to" pump out" as we had decided early on not to place unsightly portable toilets on the property, but instead open up our home and pool house, so we had to ensure that there would not be any problems during heavy use of the facilities.

We arranged to have the gardener mow the lawn on our regular Wednesday prior to the tent installation, and return on Friday afternoon after the tents were up for a last minute manicuring of the property. He also was on call for early Saturday morning, however thankfully it was not required.

The tent people were scheduled for Thursday morning, but didn't show until noon at which time eight men started carrying tent parts to the three locations that we were having covered; the rear patio for cocktails and as an inclement weather wedding site, the cooks tent for the caterers behind our easterly tree line, and of course the main tent on the lawn. It was illuminating to watch the installation (and they avoided hitting any sprinkler lines which I marked for them in advance), which took the better part of six hours.

During the tent installation, the party rental truck returned (we had sent them away in the morning as the tent people were late and we really did not want to leave the chairs, tables and other rental items, exposed to a possible rain shower) and they proceeded to bring all the rental items into the main tent. We prevailed upon them to open up the twelve tables for us so we could get a feel for the tent layout. It was not until then, that we realized that our level part of the lawn was not so level and at least six of the tables needed an "adjustment."

Paul had gone to pick up the table linens in the morning and we left them in the house until Saturday morning. I went to pick up the special beers, and we placed all the beverages into the storage shed which was placed next to the cook's tent for the caterer's convenience on Saturday morning.

Friday morning, the sound system was delivered and Paul spent two hours with the set up man to ensure that all was arranged to our complete satisfaction. We then moved the twelve boxes of predetermined table settings (all labeled and carefully wrapped) and placed them at the appropriate tables enabling the caterers to easily set up on Saturday morning.

At noon on Friday, Merriel arrived in her van with all the flowers which then needed to be taken up the hill to the pool house, where the air conditioning had been turned on two hours earlier. This was the perfect place for her to prepare the floral arrangements, and we then proceeded to carry Laura's cut crystal bowls up to her.

On cue, at 2PM, Pam the photographer arrived at the house to take some "getting ready" pictures and to familiarize herself with the property and shooting locations.

We all spent the balance of the day running last minute errands while our good friend Temi, supervised Gregg with the four hour task of decorating the tent poles; simple, but elegantly trimmed in the orange of the day.

Merriel worked until midnight, and then slept over at the cottage, and was up again at 6AM on Saturday, finalizing the arrangements. Paul and I assisted her at 7AM in placing the garland around the arch which turned out to be quite beautiful.

At 7:30AM our friend Sandy arrived to help decorate the buffet tables with the special tablecloths that Brie and Laura had selected and added some of our bird cages and cut crystal. At 8AM Temi returned to help Sandy with the project and they both finally left at 10AM to go home and change into their party clothes.

By nine we were all showered and proceeded to deal with last minute details (placing the seating arrangement cards, and last minute floral decorations).

At 9:30, Casey our dear friend and perennial Xmas party bartender arrived as she is also an accomplished hair dresser & cosmetic lady who regularly "does the bride" and she with her daughter Danielle, helped Brie, Blair, and Laura prepare for the wedding. By 9:45 I was nervous enough to call the caterer, as they had not yet arrived. The staff pulled up just as I was hanging up the phone, and they immediately set about their tasks.

By ten, I was dressed and out on the property making sure all was proceeding smoothly. At 10:45 the parking valets arrived and I reviewed the parking procedures with them as we were not allowing cars on the property.

The police chief was kind enough to assign a patrolman at the corner of Remsens Lane and 25A from 11 to 11:30AM to avoid any traffic back up on Northern Blvd.

The Kende Trio arrived at 11AM with their mom and we quickly decided on the best location for them to set up for the guest's arrival, the ceremony, and the cocktail hour.

It was now "show time" and I went out to the front entrance to greet our guests as they either walked up the driveway or arrived from the Church by van, however I was quickly ferreted away for some family wedding pictures.

I quickly returned to the patio and mingled with our guests as the ladies were busy "getting ready." The weather was perfect; about seventy eight degrees, a little cloudy (good for the photographer) with very low humidity. God had been good to Brie and we were extremely grateful as this detail, perhaps the most important of all for a garden wedding, was never within our control.

As promised, promptly at 11:30 (well maybe we were five minutes late) the short wedding procession commenced It was exactly then that I started to finally relax and enjoy the day as everything had gone smoothly and there was nothing else I could do.

The civil ceremony presided over by the Mayor was warm, personal and touching, and lasted no more than seven minutes.

Everyone then returned to the patio and enjoyed an hour of wine, champagne, and hors d'ouerves. The tables were set, the chilled soup poured and we entered the main tent at 1PM and started to have a grand time.

Everyone seemed to be relaxed and enjoying the informal setting and casual atmosphere and we could not be more pleased.

Just prior to desert, I offered my second little speech of the day and explained to everyone about my mantra for the last six weeks and of course that received a nice laugh.

As I said then, after seeing the smile on Brie's face, and the happy time that everyone was having, I knew that I would have to slightly alter the title of my memorandum:

TO

HAVING A WEDDING AT HOME... IS NOT A PARTY...

BUT IT'S WORTH IT!!!

MY 70TH BIRTHDAY CELEBRATION 2006

Although birthday parties were not high on our list, Laura and the girls insisted we celebrate my 70th as it had been thirty years since my last birthday festivity.

They asked me to decide what the celebration would be like and I opted for a day sail on a large catamaran out of St. Martin and over to Prickly Pear for snorkeling and then to Cap Juluca for a lunch on the beach at Barkley's.

I contacted the Aquamania water sports group and they informed me that their 60 ft catamaran that usually carried seventy five or so revelers would be available for a private charter on any Saturday as that was their slow day since it was the "turn over day" for time share people.

So it was that the five of us (Laura, Blair, Brie and Todd and I) sailed on this huge boat in total privacy. We laid back and enjoyed the sail over and snorkeled, swam and then headed over to Anguilla and our lunch at a lovely and casual beach front restaurant.

It was probably the most relaxed and understated B day celebration of any 70 year old and it was just what I wanted.   The sail home was magnificent and we all slept well that night for sure.

WORKING EXPERIENCES 1996- 2006

After concluding my commitment to Les Bernard in 1996, I had entered "retirement mode" and was quite content to not have any daily business obligations or pressure.

However, shortly thereafter I saw an ad in the NY Times calling for a yacht salesman for the New York boat show at the Javits Center. Since I was a boat kind of guy I thought this would be fun, so I applied to Staten Island Boat Sales, the prospective employer, and was accepted to "work" the 1997 show.

Although I did not sell a boat, they liked they way I handled myself and offered me a full time sales position in their Freeport L.I. showroom at the foot of the "miracle mile" on Woodcleft Ave. I jumped at the chance to be selling boats and just a half hour from my home so it was a perfect fit for me. Unfortunately, the sales manager there was quite possessive and wheeled and dealed so that every sale ended up being his. Since he was related to the owner, I was knocking my head against a stone wall and after a short stint, I left to once again actively pursue my retirement.

Three months later, my landscaper was sitting in my kitchen bemoaning the fact that his auto body shop business kept him so busy that he could not pay adequate attention to his landscape operation and that he was seeking a business partner to run things on a full time basis. Again, the situation appealed to me as every current customer was within ten minutes of my house, and it meant I could wear shorts and a tee shirt for the entire season, and be home whenever I needed to be, and the investment was minimal.

This worked for about two seasons and the experience was great. I learned a great deal and got a big kick out of all the clients who would say. "A Jewish landscaper??? That is something new!!" However, they sure appreciated the professional demeanor I brought to the crew and they knew if I said something would be done, it was to be and on time and within the quoted budget.

Everything was going along smoothly until my partner started to engage in some questionable financial shenanigans. I quickly found a willing buyer for the entire company, and I exited the relationship and once again "retired."

It was now 2001, and Laura was very involved with the Village having served on the zoning board and now a Trustee, responsible for the daily workings of the Village Hall.

She continuously asked me to get involved as the trustees were receiving multiple complaints about the building department and it was starting to affect the entire Village staff.

Finally in 2003, Laura was really getting upset about all the residents' complaints and she once again pleaded with me to help out. Shortly thereafter, I agreed to a consulting role in the building department, and I commenced a part time hourly position at a very modest fee.

I met with the Mayor for my marching orders and he requested that I study the department for a week or two and then make some suggestions.

Well, the very first day, I found over forty unanswered messages on the building department's message machine, some more than a week old. I immediately suggested that the current clerk be quickly replaced with someone more responsive and people oriented.

Shortly thereafter, I was given license to hire an appropriate administrative person and the rule was that all messages had to be answered daily before anyone in the department left. In two days, all the messages were up to date and that problem never reared its head again.

I spent time observing the building inspector and concluded that although he was more than proficient and knowledgeable in his "inspector role," he was not qualified to handle administrative affairs and I quickly relieved him from any 'non inspection" activity.

Within a matter of days, I had all the loose "pending files" codified and organized into three categories either awaiting CO's to be issued, zoning matters, or architectural review board pending matters.

Within another month all the old pending files had received the appropriate action and the backlog was eliminated and the department became current in its affairs.

I suggested to the Board that we hire another administrative person to share the burden as I felt the department needed five day a week coverage to remain current, as there was a definite "boom" in both old and new construction.

I started to attend all the committee meetings so that I would understand just about everything that was going on at the Village, and could then report back to the Trustees with a substantial degree of first hand knowledge.

Three months later, the Trustees asked me to become Superintendent of the Building Department, working five days a week supervising the two part time administrators, the inspector and the Code Enforcer, as most of his work was building department related. They offered me an appropriate salary and I became for the first time in my life, "a government employee." (Excluding of course my two military postings).

After accepting that role, the Mayor requested that I review every file in the village to make sure things were all ok. What I found was shocking!!!!

In the first few days I uncovered a multitude of open permits, and lack of CO's which meant an absence of inspections as well.

I then spent the better part of every day trying to review at least twenty five files, sending letters to the respective residents informing them of any open items in their files, which definitely would become an issue if and when they were seeking to add on, refinance, or sell their houses.

I urged them all to come in and find out what was necessary to bring their files up to date, and I must say most residents were quite cooperative and delighted to have their files in compliance so that they would not have any transfer problems down the road.

Those residents that resisted "cleaning" their files, ended up in court as I did have the authority to require code enforcement, and although they were not originally happy hearing from me, they finally realized that it was in their best interests to have their property up to date with current regulations.

This oversight took me the better part of a year as there were thirteen hundred files to review and the process was still ongoing when the Board of Trustees approached me to discuss yet another position within the Village.

They met only once a month and the Mayor visited the Village Hall only once a week, basically to say hello and see if there were any major problems. They all realized that the Village was growing quite rapidly and that daily oversight had become necessary just from observing the results that I had enacted in the Building Department alone.

They then asked me to accept the position of Village Administrator, working full time and supervising all of the Village employees including the clerk, deputy clerk, judicial clerk, engineer, road commissioner and code enforcer.

I attempted to run the Village as a business, with the profit motive being the peace and contentment of the residents, with a clear set of rules and lines of responsibility for the Village staff, which I must say was accomplished.

I spent about a year and a half as the Village Administrator and when the new Mayor was elected, the Village had an employee handbook, and list of procedures and practices, none of which had been in place in prior years and all matters were current.

I left the Village employ on July 1, 2006 when the new Mayor was inducted as she professed that she was going to be "a full time Mayor" and did not need an Administrator, and on that I certainly concurred.

My most significant achievement in this role was properly enforcing the 1987 New York State pool fence law. All pools built since that time required a pool enclosure if there was to be a CO issued, but there were some seventy five existing pools that predated the law and when inspected, remained improperly protected.

Every summer I read about tots on Long Island drowning in the family or neighbors pool and I never wanted to experience tragedy of that nature during my watch. I was very adamant about that, and to this day consider that my major accomplishment and contribution to the Village.

Through my vigilance and persistence, with the help of the code enforcer and the Village Justice, when I left in 2006 all but three pools had been properly protected. I have since learned that the remaining three also eventually complied.

Just for the record, when I was first employed by the Village, the Trustees had inquired about the ethics of having me on the payroll while my wife was a Trustee. The word came back from the New York State ethics committee that it was not a conflict as long as Laura recused herself from all matters regarding my employment including my salary and perks, which of course was the case.

I have now been "ungainfully unemployed" for some seven years.

BERNIE AND HIS DOGS 1944-2012

Like most young boys, I desperately wanted a dog as a companion especially since I was an only child. My folks resisted for a while but one evening in 1944 they attended a U.S. savings bond rally at the Midway theatre in Forest Hills.

Out came a young Irish Setter and to my mom's shock, my dad started to bid and he "won" the auction and for a mere $ 25,000 bond (he only had to pay ½ of that) they came home with "my" dog Kelly, a rather large Irish Setter.

I awoke the following morning and opened my bedroom door and was immediately pounced upon by this huge dog (of course any medium dog, standing on his rear paws would tower over me), and I started to scream in fear. My folks rushed in, calmed me and "introduced" me to Kelly "my" dog. I was thrilled and gave him a hug and a nice pat when I left for school. After two days, my mom said to my dad " wait a minute, you bought a dog for Bernard and every morning he leaves for school, and you leave for work and I am the one walking and caring for him." Two days later, my dad and I returned Kelly to the people that had donated him for auction. It took about four more years for me to finally acquire "my dog."

My folks determined that at twelve I should be mature enough to care for a dog and they thought that perhaps I might like to select the breed and the puppy I wanted. Hello!!! Now at least it would be "my" dog. I voted for a boxer and my dad took me to a local breeder for the selection process. He cautioned me not to show too much emotion about the puppy that appealed to me, but rather spend time petting the others puppies and in that way he could perhaps negotiate a better price.

I spotted my favorite as soon as I entered the kennel as there he was, the runt of the litter sitting alone in the corner. All the other dogs were $ 150, but the breeder said he would sell the runt for $ 75, and so we left with Mr. Runt in my arms, and I was happy as any twelve year old could be. He was a brindle with a big white patch on his chest and some white on his paws. The markings on his back gave my dad the inspiration to suggest his name as Twig and after we discussed it we decided to name "my very first own dog" Twig Beau of Wetherole, as we lived on Wetherole St.

I loved that guy and spent at least two hours every day training him to sit, stay, come, heel, lie down, play dead and give a paw. During non school hours, Twig and I were inseparable, and of course he slept in my room every night.

When I left for my freshman year in college in 1953, truthfully, I was more upset about leaving him than leaving my parents, who promised to take good care of him until I returned for vacations or for the summer months.

By then we were spending our summers in Long Beach and Twig and I spent many an early morning or early evening hour walking, running or playing catch on the beach, and he loved jumping into the waves with me. What a guy, and what a "brother" to have.

In the summer of 1954, my college friend Paul was visiting with us in Long Beach and one night when we returned from a movie, I could immediately sense the agony on my parents face as I entered the apartment and I noticed my dog was not at my feet with his stub of a tail wagging.

My parents had let him out earlier and before my dad could leash him, Twig, obviously seeing someone he thought was me, dashed across West Broadway and never saw the car, and the driver could not stop in time. Twig was mortally wounded and my dad put him into the trunk of his car and rushed him to the vet, who told him the dog was too far gone to save and recommended putting him "to sleep."

I was devastated at the news and was mourning the loss of my beloved friend, but more importantly I was also concerned for my folks who felt so guilty about being the responsible parties to the event. This was my first of many losses of a loved one, and as heartbroken as I was, I managed to put it into perspective as it was a dog not a family member. I grieved for a while, as he was "the brother I never had," but eventually accepted the inevitable. I had enjoyed six great years, training, loving and being loved by this animal, but it was time to "move on."

I did not have another dog for seventeen years!!!!!!!!!!!!!!

In 1973 when Laura and I moved into our Muttontown home, we decided that dogs were a must and we decided on Great Danes because of the size of our property. So it was that we took my two daughters to the breeder and let them each select a Dane puppy.

Brandeis (aka Brandy) and D'artagnan (aka Dart) were brothers and both fawn colored and they grew into full fledged Danes in a rather short time.

Approximately six months later, a large black dog wandered on to the property at the head of a pack of about eight dogs. At first we were alarmed, but the lead dog was so sweet and the others just followed her. The black dog was back the next day and as we got closer, we noticed she had some welts on her back, and had obviously had been abused. Laura fed her and she willingly came into the house after two days.

We then placed an ad in the NY Times as we knew if we wanted to legally keep her we had to first post a notice to see if her rightful owner would show up. For the first two days, we heard nothing and on day three we got a call from the owner (who we assumed was the abuser) so we denied housing her any more and he said "oh that is too bad as I was looking for a home for her as she is too much for me to handle and I have her papers," to which Laura quickly replied, "well if you could drop off her papers, we would make an effort to find her." He of course knew we had her, but he did drop off the papers and Princess now became our third purebred Dane.

Brandy passed away from a heart attack when he was about five and Dart followed him the following year. Princess on the other hand lived with us until she was eleven, which in Great Dane years was quite a long time. We then "rescued" Moose and Lucky from the Great Dane rescue pound, so we always had at least two Danes living with us and sometimes three. They were all big and all warm and friendly and great family dogs.

Moose was a daunting two hundred and forty pound black Dane charmer who was extremely loveable. He would come and stand in front of you, then turn around and back into your lap with his rump. It was quite a scene seeing this huge animal "sitting" on our guest's laps.

As time went by, he became aggressive with other dogs off of the property as he would "jump" our fence and invade the other dog's property and when that dog objected he would get a little feisty and on two occasions we were taken to court with a neighbor's complaint. The first time I appeared in front of the judge it was in Muttontown and although the judge praised me for my rather eloquent defense of my dog, he was convicted of being a nuisance and threat to the community and if he was to appear again on similar charges he would have to be euthanized. Gulp!!!!! We ended up spending $ 5000 to heighten our perimeter fencing all around the property and I would joke, our "free dog" was rather costly.

He found his way out once more and had a run in with another neighbors dog and he again was hauled into court, but this time it was in Brookville, and the judge had no evidence of his "prior conviction" so again Moose got off with a warning, and I paid for my neighbor to install gates on his circular driveway. The "free dog" was becoming a major expense.

Lucky passed away at six, and Moose was living with us alone, but was starting to become aggressive just when Brie and Blair were turning nine and ten respectively. One afternoon, Brie and her friend Jessie were playing and wrestling on the floor in our red den and Brie started to yell and Moose came charging in. Seeing Brie's friend on top of her, he quickly, but gently, put his enormous jaws around the poor child's head.

The girls immediately stopped wrestling and screaming and Moose backed off. Luckily for us that Jessie's parents were also dog lovers and did not pursue any action against the culprit.

Three months later, I was sitting at the kitchen table with Brie and Dara, another of her friends, when I saw Moose enter the kitchen and start to make a B line for her. I got my hand on Dara's head just as Moose started to clamp down and instead he got me.

We now were on notice that Moose must have been abused by one of the former owner's pre teen children, and was starting to relate poorly to our daughters friends.

Two days later he bit our renter, and that was more than we could take as we now knew with out a doubt that we had a keg of dynamite on our hands and we could not wait for another explosion. It was with great sorrow, but with much relief, that we proceeded to euthanize Moose. He was always my favorite Dane as he was for the first five years, a gentle giant, but we could no longer take any chances with him and his growing aggressive feelings towards people, so sadly and grudgingly we had to "put him down."

After our Great Dane years, we became enchanted with the loveable looks of the Shar Pei's that were the guard dogs of the Chinese Emperors. They were known as the "wrinkle dogs" and gained immense popularity in the U. S. in the late 80's and early 90's.

We located a U.S. breeder in Pennsylvania and between us and Laura's parents we purchased and raised four of that breed. Ours were named Ruffles, Noodles and Chop Stix and all three were adorable as puppies, but I must say as they matured they were more stand offish than our Danes and were not quite as child friendly. My in laws' male was named Bradley and although they loved him, they recognized that when he matured, he became a very aggressive male, obviously still imbued with the genes of his forbearers.

After our three passed, it was the end of dogs for the Shapiro's. The proverbial "kids had left for college and the dogs had died" rang true in our household.

The last of our dogs were our St. Martin Island Coconut Retrievers (not yet recognized by the ACC) who loved our water front ambience in St. Martin.

First there was Docker (so named as I found him wet and frazzled and undernourished under my boat dock). Over a matter of days we coaxed this part black Labrador retriever into our home and soon into our hearts.

He eventually mated with our neighbors dog Cece who gave birth to Jr. a rather large partial black Labrador that became our favorite St. Martin dog, who lived both at our house and next door with his mother Cece.

When Docker died, we went about rescuing two other local dogs, Coco and Sox. They were owned by a Belgian couple that were leaving the Island, but could not take the dogs with them. They ran "one last ad" in the local paper and luckily we noticed it, and adopted them both. They became the house dogs at Mirabelle for the remaining years of our ownership.

When we were in the midst of selling the house, we flew all four dogs from St. Martin to Muttontown. We then drove Coco and Sox up to our friends, Susan and Steven Wise in Toronto as they had rented our house on multiple occasions and loved the dogs and we just could not keep all four. (My determination, not Laura's for sure).

We did keep Junior and Cece with us. Junior (Cece's son) succumbed to cancer in the fall of 2011 and Coco passed away in Canada during the summer of 2012.

Sox is still alive and well in Canada, and Cece is still with me and we are kind of inseparable. I lost my wife and she lost her son, and the two of us have bonded.

So I have owned, trained, loved and lost a dozen or so dogs, all of whom had great and very different personalities. All have a place in my heart.

Losing a pet, although not considered a tragedy, is indeed a heartbreaker, but it is also a great life lesson, especially for young people who have to at some point in their lives, face the harsh reality of death. I know it helped me with my travails over the years and for that I am thankful.

God bless all those loveable and loyal four legged critters!!!!

BERNIE AND BOATS

By now, any of you who know me, are aware of my affinity for dogs, the water, and boats. I grew up with all of them and have kept them all in my life whenever possible. Regarding the water; I am most comfortable when I am either in it, on it, or looking at it, whenever I can.

The only one of our residences during my marriage to Laura that was not "on the water" was and is our Muttontown residence as both L.I sound and the Atlantic Ocean are miles away, but our NYC and Palm Beach apartments were water front as was our St. Martin home. I am constantly drawn to the water and panoramic views of it.

As a young boy, I remember my dad taking me fishing in a rowboat off the Far Rockaway jetties, where we fished for king fish. The boat and motor were rented from Henning's fishing stations, located just west of the Atlantic Beach Bridge, and I mention that, as years later my dad purchased Mr. Henning's personal fishing boat.

When I was around twelve, my dad, who also loved the water, "stepped up to the plate" and spent $1,750 on a Barbour fifteen foot lap strake boat with a fourteen horse power Evinrude motor. (I note here that he was nervous about powering up and buying the eighteen horse power Johnson).

It was on this small runabout that I became enamored with boating, as my dad quickly let me solo for the experience of it. We had that boat moored at the Eagle Pier in Long Beach (long since gone) and I hung around there quite a bit.

Two years later my dad purchased Frank Henning's "stripper boat" which was a solidly built twenty one ft. skiff which enabled us to do some ocean fishing as we now had a serious boat under us and my dad was starting to "feel his boating cheerios." Here I learned how to maneuver and handle a "real" boat with a ninety five horse power single screw inboard engine.

When I was about seventeen my father bought a brand new thirty foot twin screw Ulrichsen sea skiff, and now we were "really in to boating" as we could go out the Rockaway Inlet and head East while fishing and re enter thru the tricky Jones Beach Inlet. I handled this boat too, as I was now an accomplished boatman, my father having sent me to a retired captain in Freeport who gave me private "how to boat" lessons, which included all of the nautical skills needed to confidently cruise the local area.

My lessons were given both on the captain's single screw twenty foot skiff, and at his kitchen table, studying navigation, the nautical right of way, the effect of winds and currents, and boating etiquette.

My final test came when the captain called me in Long Beach one summer afternoon and said I needed to come over immediately for my final exam. I said "it is so windy out here; is it not too windy in Freeport?" He replied, "Yes the wind is blowing at twenty five miles per hour and Jones Inlet will be a bitch today and that is why you need to come over now."

A half hour later, we were heading thru Reynolds Channel and entering the infamous Jones Inlet, a body of water feared by most local boatman for its tricky currents and rough and following seas, especially on windy days.

As we approached the entrance to the inlet I asked the captain if he was sure he wanted me to pilot his boat into those waves and rollers.

He said " son, I would not recommend taking a boat out in this kind of wind and sea conditions, but one day you will invariably find yourself in just such a sea and rough conditions and you will hopefully learn today how to handle treacherous waves, currents, winds and white caps."

We entered the inlet, bobbing up and down, but heading steadily thru till we reached some calmer water about ½ mile offshore. He turned to me and said "good job young man now comes the tough part and that is turning around and getting back into the harbor without capsizing this vessel."

Was I nervous? You bet. I had no choice but to run the gauntlet through the waves, wind, and following sea, and into the harbor we sailed and back to his berth. When I docked the boat " on a dime" which was not so easy to do with a single engine boat, the captain turned to me, shook my hand and said, "Bernie you have passed "How to Pilot a Boat- School," with flying colors."

Today, as I hear of unnecessary boating tragedies, I think back in time and thank god, the captain, and my father, for my boating education.

Some years later, when I was married for the first time, my dad really stepped up to the plate and purchased a 38 ft Post, an ocean going vessel of some note with a very fine reputation for sea worthiness.

I spent a lot of time on this boat with the children of my first marriage as I tried to imbue them with the "water bug" that I had inherited from my dad.

Thankfully my father kept that boat for a number of years so that I could enjoy it with Laura too. Although she still could not swim, she loved being on the water with me as she was very comfortable with my boat handling skills and my very deep respect for the sea.

I learned early on that every boat, from that first row boat to the Queen Mary, can be reduced to a floating cork when Mother Nature exercises her will. No boat is a match for an angry sea and a good boater is a knowledgeable and respectful boater, and I do count myself as one of that number.

MY VERY OWN BOATS

While I did eventually own four boats, none of them approached the size, luxury or seaworthiness of my dad's larger vessels, but I had learned to keep it small and simple as a boat is a "bigger hole" than any house and the larger it is and the more gadgets you have on board, the more problems you will encounter and the more money it will cost.

I purchased my first vessel when newly married to Toby in 1959 and living in Freeport. It was a fifteen foot Lyman with a fifty horse power outboard and I aptly named it "True Love" (a double entendre for sure). I enjoyed fishing & boating around the Jones Beach area while we lived there, but sold it when Lauren was born and we moved to the North Shore, as infants and small boats are not really a good mix.

I purchased my second boat in 1974 when Laura and I had moved from NYC to Muttontonwn. It was a twenty four ft Chris Craft Lancer with a two hundred and forty horse power inboard/outboard. I named it the "Lauren B" after my oldest daughter Lauren Beth and we spent many hours boating not only with the kids, but also with our Danes as well. It was quite a scene transporting the dogs; not so much at the dock, but when we pulled up to a beach and we had to carry them on and off. For a few summers we kept this boat moored in Shelter Island at the Deering Harbor Inn, where we took all the kids each weekend. As the children grew and were enmeshed in their own activities, I started playing golf. We sold the boat and I remained without one for about twenty years until we built our home in St. Martin.

By then I had learned the best boat to be on was .... your friend's!!!

As our St. Martin house was under construction, I purchased a twenty four foot Boston Whaler with twin ninety five horse power Evinrude engines, and we enjoyed that boat for five years. I then sold the boat and took a boating hiatus for two seasons. By then I had determined that I wanted a small, low upkeep, inflatable, for running around Simpsons Bay. There was an Apex dealer in St. Martin who imported the boat from Costa Rica where it was manufactured. During our first visit to Costa Rica, I purchased my custom fitted twenty foot Apex inflatable with a single ninety horse power outboard, had it shipped to the dealer in St. Martin and enjoyed it for the last two years of our Island time.

NEWPORT OR BUST

I must relate a boating story to you that I experienced circa 1964, when, with my first wife, and our neighbors, Jerry and Carol Baim, we chartered a 34 ft skiff for a week of cruising on Long Island Sound.

We were en route to Newport R.I, when we ran into a major storm off of Wakefield and the Coast Guard was advising us to pull into the closest protective harbor, but we were "beyond the point of no return" and found ourselves in a rough, wind tossed following sea. I was at the helm on the fly bridge, as Jerry did not have enough experience to handle the boat under those circumstances. Carol, out of fear and desperation, chose that moment to announce she was pregnant with her third child. Oh my!!!!

I thought back to my "rite of passage" under my teacher those dozen years or so ago. All that he taught me re a following sea and windy conditions as encountered in Jones Inlet during my final exam, came back to guide us and the vessel for the next two hours, until we reached the safety of Newport where we all disembarked and "kissed the ground." It was a very rough trip!! Nothing beats knowledge and hands- on experience. I was properly taught and all my nautical "studies" had paid off in spades. I owe a debt of gratitude to my father for showing me the right way to do things!! Every time!!!

THREE FUNNY BOATING STORIES THAT I REMEMBER

Circa 1958: Long Beach NY. My dad had his 30 ft Ulrichsen skiff and we had just docked the boat at Bianca's Marina in Reynolds Channel in Island Park and were standing on the dock chatting with all the fellow boaters when we all spied a brand new Owens thirty foot mahogany planked boat heading to the dock at warp speed. Suddenly, the "captain" who was at the helm, started looking furiously around at his feet while heading directly into the dock. I said "oh my god he is looking for the brake," and a few seconds later he slammed bow first into the dock about six feet from where we were all standing. He could then be heard saying to his guests, "where the hell is the f—king brake on this f—king boat."

With that, all of us doubled up in laughter as we knew it was his maiden voyage on his new toy and he never had a minute's prior experience in piloting a boat. The story was funny, but it made me aware of the necessity of educating boaters before they injure themselves or others on board with their lack of knowledge. Sadly, even today, although we have Power Squadron courses that are helpful, there is no licensing requirement for boaters and that is something I have never understood.

Circa 2005: St. Martin. I had my twenty four foot Boston Whaler that I used to run around in Simpson Bay in St. Martin and I was so proud of how nicely the boat handled and truthfully how nicely I was able to maneuver it. (Until of course I "found" all the rocks in the lagoon on three separate locations and had to buy new props).

It was the year that the Isla Del Sol Marina was opened and all the really large yachts were coming to St. Martin for the winter season. When I say large, I mean from a hundred to three hundred feet, with Leslie Wexner's Limitless being the Queen of the fleet.

Most of the boats had "a dingy" that was as large or larger than my boat and they were housed INSIDE the yacht itself and "launched" when ever the owner wanted to visit some part of the Island.

One day, with my daughter Brie, we headed into Marigot, the capitol of the French side to the Marina Royal, as we were going into town for lunch. There was a "dingy dock" which was used mostly by the sailors that lived aboard their sail boats, as they usually came into town for supplies on a daily basis.

As we were pulling into the dock, a Frenchman looked over at us as he exited his twelve-foot rubber inflatable dingy and said to me "monsieur, this dock is reserved for dingy boats only."

Without skipping a beat, I retorted with a mild French accent: "Monsieur, this is my dingy" to which he replied "pardonez moi."

Brie almost fell over board from laughing so hard and I remember her looking at me and saying "how the hell did you retort like that so quickly?"   I said it just came up and out and we have always laughed at" Bernie's dingy" which in fact was my "yacht."

I could never have used that line if not for all the major vessels that were moored at the Isla Del Sol Marina, located at the other end of the Bay.

Circa 1955: Long Beach N.Y. I saved this story for last because it involves my dad who was the consummate boater/fisherman. One morning that summer, he wanted to take me and Paul out on his relatively new pride and joy Ulrichsen twin engine skiff. He wanted to exit via Rockaway inlet and head to the ocean fishing grounds outside of Long Beach. It was a calm, hot morning with almost no breeze and gentle rollers that the boat effortlessly glided over. He stopped the engines and we started our first drift for fluke which were running pretty well two miles offshore. After fifteen minutes, I noticed Paul sitting down in the corner of the rear deck and turning a pale green. Oh, oh for sure sea sickness was quickly overcoming him and my dad, knowing what that feels like, instantly turned the boat towards home and the trip back to port.

As we approached the inlet, my dad turned to me and said "well since you are such an accomplished boatman, would you like to take the helm and guide us back through the inlet to the channel home?"   He gave me the wheel as we entered a very calm inlet, but with a strong outgoing tide. About ten minutes into my handling of the boat we heard a big bang, the boat lurched and the props started to vibrate. Obviously I had hit something and when we looked to the stern up floated a huge waterlogged telephone poll that had been completely submerged. I had run over it and from the sound of things, I had bent both props. My dad started cursing and yelling as he felt I had been non observant and negligent in handling the boat and he grabbed the wheel and guided us back to the nearest boat yard as he knew the boat would have to come out of the water to check on the damage. He was beet red, yelling all the way in and Paul, who was still sitting on the deck floor in major distress, now also had to endure my father ranting and raving.

The props were bent and had to be replaced and the boat was laid up for a week until the new ones were delivered and installed.

My dad, for whom I was then working, did not speak to me for a month.

And I mean... did not speak to me.

One day, he had no one to join him and he said he needed me to come out with him fishing again as he didn't want to head out alone. As a dutiful son, I did.

After a fruitful few hours and a large pail full of fluke, he took us back thru the inlet with me sitting across from him. For sure he was not turning the helm over to me and that was indeed a relief. In almost the same exact spot as that fateful morning a month earlier, we again heard a loud sound and looked back and guess what? There appeared another large water soaked telephone pole as the boat started to vibrate and make familiar noises.

I looked at him, did not say a word, but then burst out laughing and he did too, as he turned beet red, but this time from embarrassment not anger.

Lesson learned—-sometimes when out on the water or, navigating yourself through life, things can happen that are totally unpredictable and unavoidable no matter how expert or diligent you are, and you always have to be vigilant (especially on the water).

My dad finally started speaking to me again, but he never admitted to anyone that he too had smacked into a submerged pole.

Until now, I never told the story to anyone except Paul…

And my mother.

CELEBRATING MY 75TH BIRTHDAY 2011

As you can well imagine, I had to think long and hard about any celebration of my 75th birthday as it would be my first since Laura had passed.

When I checked the Friends Academy vacation schedule and realized it was over the week of March 30th, the decision to take my family to St. Martin was immediate. I did have to think about the emotional stress for going there without Laura, but as I had already explained to the girls earlier, our St. Martin life really started in the late 70's with our discovery of La Samanna and the many good times we enjoyed there, both just the two of us and then with the girls and their friends.

We gravitated to La Samanna, as it was the only place in the world where Laura "came close" to relaxing as it was so simple for her to just take a chair down to the waters edge and sit in the shallows, the gentle waves lapping at her feet while she would read a book and just "come down." For someone who could not swim it was an ideal compromise.

We loved it there and when we sold Mirabelle in 2010 we discussed coming back down to La Samanna and how exciting it would be with our grandchildren. I know that is exactly where she would have wanted us to come to celebrate our 39th anniversary and my 75th birthday.

So that is where we headed and the celebration was memorable because of the lovely week I spent there with the kids and for an intimate birthday celebration dinner at Bamboo Bernie where we were joined by my friends, Joanna and Larry Lesser and Ardith and Charles Mederrick.

It was low key, private and very sentimental, as we did bring down a crystal domed butter dish that Laura loved, and it was placed on the table signifying her presence, a tradition that we have, and will continue to follow, on all family celebration occasions.

I suspect that may well be my last birthday "gala" unless I make it to my 100th in 2036.

BERNIE AND BOLLYWOOD

After a respectful mourning and grieving period, I decided that it was time to once again "move on," and I informed my closest friends that I was ready to socialize in a limited understated way. The very first meaningful invitation I received to mingle came in mid September 2010 from my friends Temi and Ronnie Birnbaum, who invited me to a pre Yom Kippur dinner at their home. They assured me it would be a very low key evening as the only other guests would be their son Todd and his wife.

With that assurance, I accepted. During our rather private dinner, Todd received a text/email, and after reading it he said, "Bernie this is really a message for you." Bewildered, I asked him what the hell he was talking about and he related that his friends, Lisa and Debbie Ganz who owned Twins World, a New York based casting company, were "Seeking highly opinionated seniors with tons of personality, who are ready to remind America what it's like to be mature, wise and full of life experience." They had received a call from LA. as there was a TV reality show in the making that was going to focus on celebrating the lives and experiences of seniors, and Todd thought I would be a great candidate.

I told him he was crazy and that I had no interest, but he insisted on forwarding the email to me so I could review it when I arrived home. The next morning I did just that, and encouraged by my daughter Blair, I filled out the application form answering all the questions as best as I could. She suggested that she review my answers before I emailed them to Twins World, as she wanted to perhaps "sharpen" some of my responses and make them, more appropriate, up to date, and zippier, which she did.

A few days went by, and truthfully I forgot all about the situation. I was in the midst of cleaning up the attic when the phone rang and Blair answered it, and I heard her say (in a voice loud enough for me to hear) "yes Debbie, my dad is here and I will get him on the phone." I came down and spoke with Debbie for about forty five minutes, and honestly I had her in stitches almost the whole time until she finally said, "Bernard, we need you to come in next week for an audition tape that we will be sending out to LA. as you seem perfect for the show."

I hung up the phone kind of stunned and Blair said, "dad you were great and I know you are what they are looking for, but please let me dress you for the taping." I said of course as I knew she was so style savvy. She insisted that I wear my lace-less sneakers which I thought was crazy, but I caved and wore exactly what she laid out for me; jeans, a nice shirt with one of my cool sweaters and of course the lace- less sneakers.

When I was taken into the taping studio and the cameras were rolling the very first thing that Lisa said to me was; "wow those are cool sneakers for a man of your age," and that set the tone for a great thirty minute taping episode. The only question that I could not answer properly was, "Bernard do you know what metro sexual is?" I thought about it for a moment and replied, "I am not sure, but it sure sounds like sex in the subway," which cracked her and everyone else in the room up. I have since learned the meaning of the term and realize that I am surely a metro sexual guy, as I am somewhat fastidious about my appearance.

After the taping I was told it would be sent out to LA. and I would hear if there was any further interest. Three weeks later I received a call from Kerry Shanahan, the casting coordinator of 3 Ball Productions in LA., letting me know how excited they were about what they saw on my audition tape, and she wanted me to know when the final selection process would take place and what the schedule would be like. She ended her e mail by saying "Hopefully you are just as excited as we are for what could possibly be the ADVENTURE OF A LIFETIME."

I will admit that I then became quite excited too, as this would be just a perfect first journey for me, helping me "move on" some six months after Laura's passing. Two weeks later, Melanie Oncley, another casting coordinator, sent me a "background check application" to fill out and return, and then on November 3rd, she also sent me eleven very relevant personal questions which she said she needed answers to. In addition I was sent a W-9 form to fill out for tax purposes, as successful finalists would be paid a daily stipend of $ 150.

On November 13th I was told that I was still one of the top favorites and that I would need to undergo a comprehensive psychological and medical examination, and if I "passed" those tests, I would be flown out to LA. for a final network inter- view.

However on the 16th, I received notice that I had been eliminated from the final interviews and the process was to be terminated. Upon receiving that news, I was quite disappointed, as by then I was really looking forward to visiting LA. for the final audition. Two days later I received a frantic call on my cell phone that I was "reinstated," and I needed to have my two tests completed in the next day or two.

On the 19th, after completing my two evaluations, I was notified that I had been accepted, and was one of ten finalists from the nine thousand applications they had reviewed, and that I should be making plans to head out to LA. right after Thanksgiving.

Well, at this point I was really "getting into it," and I told most of my close friends what was happening. Of course everyone wanted me to make the final cut so they could see me make an ass of myself in a nationally televised HBO reality show, but I could tell they really were rooting for me as it would be a great first adventure after Laura's passing, and everyone thought it would be good for my head.

Shortly thereafter, I was told I would be flying out to LA. on the 29th, and that the FINAL network interview would take place on the 30th and five of us would be selected and the other five would be sent home. I was told to pack for three weeks of shooting, since if selected, I would be there from Dec. 2nd to the 20th, sequestered in the production site with no outside communication allowed. The next day, Blair and I went to Saks Off, and she supervised the purchase of my reality show wardrobe.

I was cautioned not to speak to anyone on the plane about why I was flying out to LA. as the show was "highly confidential???" Upon arrival at the LA. airport, I was chauffeured to the Ayres Hotel in Hawthorne and taken to my room and sequestered until escorted by one of the casting crew to the dining room, where I was to dine alone.

After dinner I was summoned to a meeting room where I met the other finalists. I must say they were certainly a bunch of characters, some from the Big Apple, some from Texas, and some from the Mid- West. I was certainly " the most normal" of all of them, and right then I knew the type of people they were seeking for the show, and realized that my persona did not exactly fit the bill, but that would be up to the network honchos.

The following morning I was again escorted throughout the hotel and finally taken to the final screen test room, with the TV cameras in my face. I was told that the network executives were in the adjoining room, monitoring the interviews, to determine who would make the final cut.

The casting director started to ask me various disconnected questions and then finally she asked, "Why do you think you should be on the show?" I responded that not knowing exactly what the show was about, I could only say that if they were looking for an articulate, sophisticated, well traveled, low key type, who could bring wisdom and reason to the show, then I was their guy, but if they were seeking "loonies" to yell and scream to create havoc on the show, then I was not their man.

I was then told "thank you," and escorted back to my room to await the final word on whether or not I had made the final cut.

Now I must digress here and tell you that my friend Ardith Mederrick had mentioned that she had a lady friend she thought I should meet while out on the coast, and she gave me Sandy's phone # just in case I had some free time to call her.

At about 5 PM, the casting team came up to my room to inform me that they were heartbroken, but the network had not selected me for the show and I would be going back to NYC in the morning. They then said they would be back later to escort me to dinner, as I was still to be kept apart from any of the other finalists.

After they left, I called Sandy and asked if she was free that evening, but I explained that I could not drive up to see her as I was really sequestered in the hotel. Being a good sport, she volunteered to drive down from her apartment in Santa Monica, and that we could eat at the bar in the hotel. I said that would be great.

When my still disappointed casting buddies came up to escort me to dinner, I informed them that I had a date that was driving down to dine with me. They were flabbergasted and asked "how did you line up a date in such a short time?" I replied, "Hey, do you think I would come all the way out here without a plan B?" They all laughed and promised to give us some privacy at the bar.

Sandy did in fact drive down and she was charming. We had a great conversation as she related some of her dating experiences, and advised me how much easier it would be for me to date widows rather than divorcees as I would have more in common with them. I then told her that I had experienced both being divorced and now being a widower, so I "was ready for all comers."

I retired to my room and the next morning was escorted to the airport and home. I returned, not having made my mark in Bollywood. I had a lot of disappointed friends, but there were two people that were delighted that I did not make the cut. Both Blair and Brie were cringing that their dad would make a jack ass of himself on a nationally televised reality show, so they were happy campers.

It was a very interesting two months and just another one of my many varied meaningful life experiences as it gave me the impetus, upon returning home, to start dating and "moving on" into the last quadrant of my life.

To my knowledge, the show never made it to the small screen, so I guess in retrospect, all worked out just fine as no doubt it was not in the cards for me to become a TV celebrity.

However, I did get to keep my Saks wardrobe of stylish jeans and T shirts.

POST SCRIPTS TO THE ADDENDUMS

I hereby, once again, respectfully invoke my requested poetic license to insert some of my disjointed quasi articulate ramblings, as I felt they just did not lend themselves to any particular chronological placement.

PING PONG, EXERCISE, RACQUETBALL AND SWIMMING 1943- 2012

When I was five and we moved to Rego Park there was both a ping pong and pool table in the basement of the apartment building, and it was here that I learned my skills at those games, with ping pong being by far my favorite of the two.

I honed my table tennis ability over the years playing here and there socially with friends or hotel guests when on vacation, but it was during my Army years that I really sharpened my game and became the battalion champ on two occasions, and to this day I do play a better than average social game. I find it interesting that just recently a series of ping pong parlors have opened in downtown New York and I am looking forward to visiting them as soon as it is convenient. No not to play, but just to observe, as my very rudimentary defensive game will be no match for the "pros" that are now wielding the paddles and "cutting and slicing" the ball.

When I was discharged from the Army in 1959, I was in pretty good shape from the rigors of basic training and my regimen thereafter, and when we moved to Roslyn I continued jogging and even organized some of my neighbors to join me. I also became a life time member of Vic Tanney and was lucky enough to have North Shore Health Club honor my membership when they took over his facility in the Miracle Mile when he went bankrupt. I did work out religiously, but truthfully, I found exercise very boring and I always felt that the best part of the workout was the sauna and steam room. I continued my exercise regimen for many years, both in NYC and Long Island and gave up many lunches in Manhattan for a one hour workout, but I never really enjoyed the gym and it was not until I was introduced to racquet ball in the early 70's that I truly found an exercise I enjoyed.

I embraced the game, taking lessons from pros and playing both singles and doubles for the next 35 years and truly deriving pleasure from competing against much younger participants while keeping up my cardio fitness.

I played the game until I was 70 and my left knee "waved the white flag of surrender," and I elected not to have surgery, but to just give it up and concentrate on my swimming.

From the time I was five, swimming has always been in my life either in Far Rockaway, Miami, Atlantic Beach, Long Beach, and St. Martin or any where I was on vacation. I love the water, and as you all know by now, I am quite comfortable in it, on it, or viewing it. Swimming is an exercise that can be carried throughout life at many different levels, and I look forward to enjoying both pool and ocean swimming in my remaining years.

Hopefully as you will discover in my last chapter, I will eventually reside in Long Beach, and when the boardwalk is restored, I anticipate that I will add walking and bicycling to my exercise regimen.

LAURA MOVES IN WITH ME   1970

I am not sure how I can adequately explain what I am about to say, but I will just try to relate it as it happened. You just had to be there to appreciate the hilarity of the situation.

Laura and I were getting quite serious in our relationship and the lease on her Flushing apartment was about to expire and we decided (actually she decided and I concurred) that it would make no sense for her to renew, but rather move in with me in NYC. To expedite the "move in," we rented a van and drove out to Flushing and the two of us schlepped some of her furniture and clothing down the elevator and loaded it into the van. We then drove into Manhattan and unloaded the van taking everything up to my apartment and appropriately placing it.

When we were finished, I said, "OMG, my housekeeper is coming in tomorrow and since she also works for my parents, she will tell them you have moved in with me before we have alerted either of our parents about the seriousness of our relationship, and that will really upset them."

Let us not forget this was some forty two years ago and although I was thirty five and Laura was twenty eight, you did not just casually "move in together." At least not in our families.

She looked at me and we both started to laugh as we proceeded to take everything back down the elevator and into the van for the ride back to Flushing, where we took everything back up to her apartment. We drove back to the city, returned the van, and collapsed.

When she told her mother what we had done, she became hysterical laughing and said "you mean Mr. Bernard of Les Bernard actually rented and drove a van??? Why should we care?? You two are adults…."

Four months later, in March of 1971, we were married.

I was much to embarrassed to ever tell my parents the story!!!!

LAUREN AND THE SEACREST DINER CAPER -1982

When my eldest daughter Lauren came home from Drake for the summer, one of our friends who was a regular at the Seacrest Diner managed to secure her an interview with Nick Bouloukos the diner's owner. He immediately hired her as a hostess and asked her to start the very next day, May 29th, 1982.

The only family member that expressed displeasure was Laura's mom, who said "how can you let your daughter work at night in a diner?" We replied almost in unison that the diner was on Glen Cove Road in Old Westbury, an upscale area, and only a fifteen minute ride from the house and she would be home by twelve. Neither of us could understand why she was so concerned.

Lauren took our station wagon and reported for work at 5 PM and we settled in for the evening. I awoke at 2 AM in a start and noticed that her room was unoccupied and the car not in the courtyard. I immediately called the diner and the phone was answered by a police sergeant. When I inquired about my daughter, he told me there was a robbery at the diner and he could not give me any further information.

Ten minutes later, Laura and I were speeding down Glen Cove Road when in the distance we noticed an abundance of red flashing lights. As we approached the diner we noticed at least twelve to fifteen Nassau County Police cars and emergency vehicles including a crime scene van.

I parked and ran to the front of the diner and explained to the officer that my daughter was the hostess and I wanted to come in and verify that she was alright. I was denied admittance to the "crime scene" and was told to wait at the front door. The first victim to exit was a gentleman with a bandaged head who indicated to us that there was an armed robbery and rape that had just taken place, and he was the first victim medically attended to and released.

I again pleaded with the officer for admittance and he then did allow me entry. To my relief I saw my daughter sitting down and apparently unharmed. She was visibly shaken and after a few minutes she was permitted to leave with us.

When we arrived home, she related that about 9PM, five African American men entered and as she approached to seat them, they brandished weapons and told her to get into the other room and on to the floor. She and all the other diners were told to disrobe and put all their money and jewelry on to one of the tables. She panicked, took off her clothes, but took her new diamond studs (her 21st birthday gift from us) and swallowed them instead of "giving them up."

The eighty or so people were than kept hostage for over an hour as the robbers gathered the valuables and proceeded to pistol whip some of the patrons and rape one of the waitresses.   In the words of the lead Detective, J. F. Nolan, "Nothing in all his career years compared to the magnitude of the crime and the acts of pure evil." He added, "This was degradation of a scale that was barbaric." *In retrospect...* *"Grand mother knew best."*

The next day we learned that the gang, led by the Williams brothers had stolen a Cadillac in Brooklyn, had driven to Plainview where they invaded a home party and robbed and raped, and performed other unspeakable acts of violence. When they were finished there, they "happened" on the Seacrest as they noticed the windows were "stained" so that you could not see in or out, and that was perfect for what they had in mind.

Two days later Nassau County Police called and asked if we would allow Lauren to come in to identify the perpetrators as they had arrested all five of them. We of course said yes, but were a little concerned when they then told us she would have to go to the police precinct where they were being held and that was in Bedford Stuyvesant in Brooklyn.

All of us, including other victims, were then driven by van under police protection to the station house. Just the specter of driving thru Bed- Stuy was in itself extremely unsettling as it resembled a war zone with burnt out cars, and boarded up buildings…... Truly frightening to us from the suburbs.

We were all seated in an ante room, when a group of heavily jeweled African Americans were brought in and when I objected to them in the same room as my daughter, I was informed " those gentleman are not the criminals." "They are also victims who have come in to ID. the culprits." Apparently, I was guilty of racial profiling way back then.

As it turned out, a taxi driver that had come into the diner for directions, was able to positively identify the five men, so Lauren never had to endure a line up which would have been an additional trauma.

Two days later, Lauren picked herself up and to her credit, "got back on the horse," as she want back to the job and finished the summer working there without incident, and Laura "recovered" the swallowed diamond studs.

All of the criminals were convicted and sent to prison for anywhere from fifteen years to life, as two of them were also convicted of prior murders.

After five years, we started to receive letters at home from the parole board asking the family to comment on the upcoming parole hearings for the two Williams brothers. Of course we asked that they remain incarcerated for the full term of their sentences, but I have since learned that one was released in 2002 and the other in 2010. I believe the third person, is still incarcerated as are the two murderers.

YOU CAN NOT MAKE THIS STUFF UP.

I have often wondered what else the good lord has in store for me regarding the three children of my first marriage. Marc has been permanently incapacitated. Elissa had allegedly been abused by her step father, and Lauren was a traumatized victim of "the greatest criminal rampage in Nassau County history."

My son is unable to communicate with me and my two daughters have chosen not to......... Enough already!!!!

THE ENRON DEBACLE

It was around 1961 and I was twenty five when my dad started buying me stock in a company called Northern Natural Gas. I was too young and unsophisticated to be dabbling in stocks, but since the 500 shares were a gift, who was I to quibble. The physical stock certificates went into the vault as I certainly did not have a brokerage account back then.

The following year the stock split two for one and a few years later the company was sold to an energy firm. After a couple of subsequent mergers and acquisitions, the stock I owned was in a gas company called Enron and the shares still stayed in my vault. Enron then over the years split again and again so I had 4000 shares as did my dad. He often talked about selling his shares, but I convinced him to hold on as it was paying a nice dividend. By then I was financially astute enough to have a brokerage account at Prudential and my shares were transferred from my vault to my stock account.

When my dad passed away in 1987 I inherited his 4000 shares and now had 8000 shares and the stock was selling at about $ 25 a share where it had languished for some time. It was worth about $200,000 which was not a bad sum, but hardly a fortune. Soon thereafter the stock started to gain in value and the shares split again and I had 16,000 shares and the stock was trading in the mid 40's's and worth about $ 650,000 and still paying a nice dividend. A year or two later the stock was selling in the mid 60's and I was delighted at my rising net worth.

In the late 1990's Enron was becoming a powerhouse in the natural gas industry and was voted "the best company in America to work for" three years running, and Forbes named it "America's most innovative company" for six years running. I was delighted to have such a substantial investment in an industry leader.

By the year 2000 Enron was barreling along and was a darling of Wall Street and sales and profits were skyrocketing. The shares again split 2 for 1 and I now had 32,000 shares of a stock that was selling in the high 80's and it sure dramatically increased my net worth.

The "high tech bubble" had just taken a lot of investors to the cleaners as huge sums of money were lost when many of those companies were shown to be empty shells and hardly worth anything close to what they were selling at. Enron, on the other hand, was a "rock solid" model employer with soaring sales and profits and the stock was now priced in the 90's and my dear friend Paul was urging me to sell stock and take some money off the table. I told him I was holding out for a few more points and at 100 I would start an orderly liquidation of my shares which were now worth over $ 3,000,000. The stock hit a high of ninety five, and then the "shit hit the fan" and Enron was exposed as a total fraud and the stock plummeted.

I remember going into my brokers office at Prudential on 9/10/01 with Paul, and sitting by a "real time" screen watching the shares lose value and my net worth start to rapidly dwindle. I sold most of my shares on the way down, but at markedly lower prices than the all time high it had peaked at. Coincidentally, the very next day was the infamous 9/11 so irreverently speaking; the only thing that went down quicker was the Twin Towers. I never really lost out of pocket money in the stock as I owned it so inexpensively, but I took a hit of over $ 2,000,000 to my net worth. Ken Lay, the Chairman, died of a heart attack a few years later after being convicted of fraud thereby "escaping" any jail time, but the President, Jeffrey Skilling, did go to jail and I believe is still justifiably incarcerated.

I felt miserable for myself, but even more so for those thousands of Enron employees that lost all of their pension money that they were urged to invest in the company over the years. They were totally wiped out. I was guilty of being a little piggish by not selling some of my many shares when the stock was on the way up, but hey I was told by Wall Street that I owned one of the "finest companies in the world." It was just a few years later that Bernie Madoff was found guilty of a massive Ponzi scheme when all his investors thought they were part of one of "the finest investment companies." I learned a valuable lesson, perhaps a little too late in life to do anything about it. I eventually consoled myself by referring to one of my favorite sayings.

If wealth is lost, nothing is lost. If health is lost, something is lost.
If character and integrity are lost, than all is lost

Shame on me for my naivety and poor judgment!!!

WHITE WATER RAFTING WITH THE POKER BOYS
1988—1994

My fascination for the water led me to explore the possibility of experiencing white water rafting. I did some research and in 1990 I booked a trip out West on the Colorado River as I was being joined by my buddy Paul and my Army friend Ira, both of whom were living on the West Coast. I also invited my son in law, Larry, as I thought it would be a great bonding opportunity and he was willing to fly out from Florida, especially as the trip "was on me." Paul and Ira both opted out of the trip at the last minute for personal reasons, but Larry and I did meet up in Grand Junction, stayed overnight and were escorted the next morning to the launch site for a two day rafting adventure. It was a class IV rapids trip with # I being the smoothest and # V being the toughest. Larry was a Jewish Florida red neck that was used to the great outdoors as evidenced by his barehanded capturing of a local snake that was scaring the hell out of our fellow rafters at the overnight campsite. The water was "up" and the trip was great, and I promised myself that I would pursue additional rafting trips before my age precluded me from this kind of activity.

And so it was about two years later that I finally aroused enough interest in my poker group to schedule ten of us for a similar adventure out West. Arranging a trip like this for ten men was in itself a logistical feat, but my organizational skills prevailed, and so it was that we all flew out to Colorado for what turned out to be a great experience for all.

Upon arrival that first evening, after dinner, of course there was a traditional poker game which ended early as we had a 5 AM wake up call for our bus ride to the launch site. After a half hour of instruction, we embarked in our two rafts for a quiet hour of river floating. Then we pulled over to the river bank and the instructors informed us that the roughest part of the rapids were just ahead, and we should make sure all our belongings were securely tied to the fittings on the raft. We all thought "no big deal." We then rounded the bend and OMG; we were greeted by humongous white water waves and a raging current and the boats quickly filled with water and our female instructor yelled out, "bail or die," and that was enough for all of us to hear, so we bailed our asses off lest we perish at the very onset of our adventure.

All of my belongings were ripped from the boat and I watched helplessly as my water proof bag containing my clothes, glasses and medication were all caught up in the ripe tides. I was told not to worry as hopefully it will all be waiting for me down stream.

We finally made it through the first rapids into calmer water and yes my little pack was floating near the shoreline so my "trip was saved." That night, after a few more rapids, we finally made shore and set up camp which was no more than a couple of pup tents or just plain sleeping bags under the stars. Now at this point after running the rapids and being exposed to the sanitary facilities, one of the poker players, who shall remain nameless, offered the tour director $ 5000 if he would please call in a medical evacuation helicopter to take him back to the motel. Of course that never happened and all ten Jewish "outdoorsmen" survived the night, the next day and the trip home. I will say that one of us almost didn't make it as he was playing gin rummy with a fellow from another group and he was caught cheating, and we all had to apologize for him in order to get him "out alive." He too shall remain nameless, but we all know who the cheater was. What happens on the River stays on the River. He was eventually booted from our poker game, as he was caught "stacking the deck."

The group really enjoyed the trip and the bonding experience to the point that they asked me to organize another rafting trip two years later, but they gave me my marching orders: "Closer to home, and no overnight on the river." It turned out I did find a day trip for us on the Penobscot River in Maine and pretty much the same group flew up to Portland where we were picked up for an hours drive to the Northern Outdoors rafting site, where I had managed to rent two comfortable cottages for our two night stay (which of course included poker games each evening). We only rafted for a day, again in # IV rapids, and returned back to camp for dinner and poker and more comfortable overnight accommodations. The same fellow who offered the $ 5000 to be flown out the first time, made this trip too, but on the morning of the launch, he decided to stay in the cabin and read?????

So all in all I enjoyed three trips, but the truth is that I had a fourth trip that pre-dated the above three, and that was an initial day trip thru the Learning Annex that took me to the Leigh River in Pennsylvania. I never told anyone about that as it was just a # II rapids and just whetted my appetite for the "real thing." Again what happens on the River stays on the River.

ST MARTIN WITH THE POKER PLAYERS AND WIVES
1996- 1998

If you think making reservations for ten men for white water rafting is a logistical nightmare, try making arrangements for five of those same men, but this time with five wives.......... Sacre bleu!!!

Interest in St. Martin grew when word got out that Laura and I had purchased waterfront property. We normally did not like to travel in a group, but we were delighted when asked to book a villa for five of the poker couples, namely, Temi and Ronnie Birnbaum, Terry and Jeff Greenstein, Judy and Jerry Friedman, Lorraine and Marvin Baron and us. We booked Serena, a five bedroom beach front villa that our favorite architect, Joel, had constructed a few years earlier, and at the time was certainly one of the premier Carimo rental properties. A few of the women were skeptical and expressed displeasure in not being involved in choosing the villa we were to stay in. Thankfully, Lorraine (who had been at our home for many of our holiday parties) said, "If Laura and Bernie are booking this particular house, then I have full confidence that we will all like it."

Two of the highlights I remember were a water polo match that pitted Ronnie and me against Marvin and Jerry. Now that is like the David and Goliath story as we were greatly out weighed and much smaller in size. We fought like hell but to this day Ronnie claims he "almost drowned" from their sheer size which had us submerged most of the time. That was only the first time Ronnie "drowned," but the second instance was for real. We both enjoyed a side by side parasail ride over Orient Beach and when they "let us down," Ronnie claims we were about three feet short of touching bottom and he truly needed Jerry to swim out and help him to shore. Where the hell was I? Watching I guess. But all's well that ends well.

One of the fun things was Marvin carrying on about the pot roasts Laura had schlepped down from NY. One of the non fun things was being robbed in the middle of the night by one of the daytime maids who must have entered our rooms while we were sleeping, and stole watches and cash from all of us who were too naïve to lock our doors. It was a small blip in an otherwise perfect week.

Over all, we spent a glorious week there, swimming, sunning, eating, playing poker, all climaxed by a catered dinner feast on the last night with a three piece Caribbean steel band to add to the festivities. That evening when we were seated, I was next to Lorraine who was wearing a lovely pair of earrings that I recognized. I complimented her on them and asked whose they were and she had no clue. I asked her to please take one off and see if there was a "signature." She turned one over and said, "Oh my God, it says Les Bernard," which of course I already knew.

As I have always maintained, seeing a woman wearing a signature piece of Les Bernard was priceless, and it "made" my evening.

Two years later, all five couples, plus Mary and David Feldman and Diane and Bob Rosenberg agreed to another adventure. We re rented Serena and the villa Interlude next door, so all seven couples frolicked for a week in the sun highlighted by a terrific scavenger hunt that ended up in Orient Beach for dinner. Each of four cars were driven by one of the men who had either two or three assistants on board as we traversed the Island seeking all the objects that had been laid out for us back in New York by Steve Kess who unfortunately could not join us for the trip.

Although we all did well, first prize went to Jerry's team which included Laura and Jeff, but the prize for creativity went to Temi for her bare buns picture. The rest of us managed to take pictures of some naked rear ends at the nude beach, but Temi went and got a hamburger bun, opened it up, and took a picture of that. Now that was certainly thinking outside of the box.

We all agreed that both trips were a ton of fun, including Laura's pot roast and other offerings and these are the only times that Laura and I traveled with a group............. and I must say it was a unique experience.

BLAIR AND BRIE – BIRTHS, NAMINGS, AND MORE

I am close to concluding my numerous vignettes with some stories about Blair and Brie, their respective. births, naming, and growing up.

Laura developed a serious case of toxemia while pregnant with Blair and consequently her blood pressure was closely monitored. On the afternoon of November 30, 1973 she complained of chest pains and her Dr. asked her to meet him at North Shore Hospital, where he quickly admitted her when he discovered that her pressure was alarmingly elevated. When I spoke to her she requested I stop at the deli and bring her a nice thick corned beef sandwich. As I entered her room and started to unwrap the tasty morsel, her Dr. entered and said "ok that's it you are going to the delivery room right now." We both asked why, and he said that her pressure was so elevated that the baby was in jeopardy and time was of the essence as he felt that he might have to perform an emergency cesarean that evening. He asked me to go to the waiting room and that he would keep me updated as the situation progressed. About an hour later he came out and said that both Laura and the baby were in distress and he had no choice but to "take the baby" now even though it was two months before her due date, and he cautioned me that possibly neither she nor Laura may survive the procedure.

As you can imagine, I was not a happy camper since once again just six years after Marc's accident, I was back in North Shore Hospital facing a life threatening situation. Thankfully at 11 PM the Dr. informed me that all went well and mother and child had survived and were doing well. He did note however that the baby weighing in at 2.9 lbs would stay in the nursery for anywhere from six to eight weeks. He also informed me that due to the very early nature of her birth, that her immune system may not have had time to develop properly and that might very well rear its ugly head in the way of health problems in her later life. I hugged him, slumped down in a chair, crying like a baby, but relieved that both Laura and Blair were fine. It then dawned on me that it was still November 30th and that Blair and Marc would forever share that birthday. She, like Marc, had blonde hair and blue eyes (the only two of my five children to possess those two qualities). It was just another incident in my life that allowed me a glimpse into the mysterious ways in which god's universe works.

When it came time to sign her birth certificate, it was a no brainer as we had determined in advance that our first daughter would be named Blair Heather Shapiro. We lived across the road from the Blair Estate and Laura fell in love with the sound of that name. As a coincidence, we did get to visit with them a few years later, as Mrs. Blair was Mary McFadden's mother and of course I had a close working relationship with Mary so she invited us over for cocktails one day when she was visiting her mom.

Brie's birth by comparison was a "piece of cake" as it was a scheduled caesarian without any complications, and I was thankful for that as I was not sure that I could endure another calamitous situation. However, when I was asked to sign the birth certificate for Brie Danielle, I unknowingly spelled it incorrectly as Laura would have wanted a Bree, but the deed was done and apparently never worth undoing.

It was not until Brie was about twenty and in college that she happened to see the movie Klute, and for the first time in her life, discovered that she was named after Jane Fonda's role in that movie, Bree Daniels, who just happened to be a prostitute of some note. Brie was at first upset with us when she came upon the facts, but soon learned to laugh at the story and accepted her naming procedure. To mollify her I always said I would get her a vanity plate for her car that said "FROMAGE," but she repeatedly declined the offer.

Back in the early 70's Blair and Brie were somewhat unusual names and we received many compliments, but of course no one really knew the facts until they became our friends and inquired about the origins and Laura gladly explained her unique baby naming procedures.

To the best of our calculations, both girls were conceived out of the country; Blair in Taormina, Sicily and Brie in Paris, so they were both imbued with an international spirit so to speak, from the very inception of their respective lives.

Unfortunately, my mother passed away when Brie was only one, and Blair two, so neither of them really got to know her, but fortuitously they had Laura's mom to fill the grandma role and she performed it superbly.

Grandma and Grandpa Martin were the designated baby sitters whenever Laura and I traveled even though we had competent live in help. With out them always "being available" it is doubtful Laura would have made all those many overseas trips with me, so we were always grateful for their willingness to stay with the girls while we traveled. Of course this resulted in both girls developing a very close relationship with Grandpa John and Grandma Laura, a connection that lasted up until the very end.

On the other hand, my dad was already living in Florida when my mom passed, so his exposure to the girls was pretty much limited to our Florida trips or on one of his infrequent visits back to New York.

The Martins were happy to "sit the girls" as they were their only grandchildren and they were delighted that it gave their daughter an opportunity to become a globe trotter as up until our marriage she had only been as far afield as Puerto Rico.

When Blair turned five, we were faced with a decision as to whether to send her to the Brookville School, up the block from our home, or to private school. After examining all of our options, we made a decision to enroll her in Greenvale, in spite of admonitions from all of our friends that it was much to much of a WASP school for our girls. Laura and I decided that the polished gym like floors, and well behaved and well dressed young girls and boys, and the sterling educational reputation of the school, far outweighed the unbalanced ethnic enrollment.

Both girls attended Greenvale, Blair until the 8th grade when all of her friends left for boarding school, and Brie until 9th grade as most of her classmates stayed for the last year. The two of them always stood out not only for their names back then, but for the way Laura dressed them… straight out of the finest children's boutiques in Paris. Their appearance never went unnoticed either by other parents or the teaching staff.

Blair worked diligently to maintain decent grades in the demanding atmosphere, whereas Brie never seemed to crack a book. Here were two daughters with the same parents and upbringing, yet miles apart in their looks, demeanor, and attitude and to this day the difference is blatant.

They both went on to high school at Friends Academy and Laura and I never once regretted our decision as we felt they both received outstanding educational experiences at both schools.

Blair graduated from Boston University majoring in hospitality and today she is an excellent chef both in preparation and presentation. Additionally, she is a law school graduate. Although she never really professed any real interest in practicing, I know the legal education she received has been helpful to her thought process on many occasions. She is now a certified Shaman/ energy healer and a nutritionist who has combined her culinary skills with healthy food preparation, diet regimen and spirituality. Although she has had a number of serious boy friends, she remains single, still seeking that "right man."

Both girls spent college semesters abroad, Blair experiencing Paris as an intern at the St. James Club and Brie in Tours immersed in the local French culture.

Brie graduated from Bucknell and pursued her Masters at C.W. Post and is now a well loved and respected fifth grade math and French teacher at Friends Academy. She is married to her high school sweetheart, Todd Kraska, and they have two wonderful children, Marley Sage (5), and Luca Bernard(3 ½), both of whom are enrolled at Friends Academy in pre K and nursery school respectively.

The girls were the focus of Laura's life and they had an extremely close relationship which has made Laura's untimely demise, understandably, a difficult situation for them to handle.

As a single dad, I have tried my best to fill the void, but I know in my heart that I fall quite short, yet I keep on trying.

Yes indeed I "lost" two daughters from my first marriage, but I have been blessed with two more loving ones, with whom I have shared many happy and tender moments.

SOUTH BEACH, & CAMP KENMONT, KENT CONN. CIRCA 1943-1949,

How fitting that my very last vignette should be my earliest significant childhood memories which were just recently brought to my consciousness as I drove home on December 9th, 2012 after dropping Blair at LGA for her flight to South Beach in Miami.

Yes, I was at the Drake Hotel on Ocean Drive back in 1943 … indeed quite a bit before it became THE "South Beach." Obviously I was somewhat ahead of the curve back then.

I was seven (almost eight) and in mid February was treated to an overnight ride on the Silver Meteor which emanated from Pennsylvania Station and ended up in Miami after a twenty six hour jaunt. My folks were taking me to the Drake for a vacation before my dad was due to report for active duty in World War 11. While there he contracted pneumonia and was granted time to recover. If my memory serves me correctly, about a month later his local draft board decided that hardship deferments due to dependent children were appropriate, so he never had to report. I have always wondered if his sickness was "an act of god" or did my dad possess some advance intelligence that guided him to seek a few weeks excuse. In today's military parlance, "I never asked, and he never told."

At any rate, I was in third grade and since my mom and I were scheduled to stay for two months, I was enrolled in the Mannheim private school so that my "education would not be interrupted." I distinctly remember being awakened each weekday morning at 7:30 and descending by myself to the dining room, where I ate breakfast under the watchful eyes of the dining room staff who then escorted me out front to catch my 8:15 mini bus to school.

There were only two other children in my class, so in effect I was receiving private tutoring even at that early age. The results were blatantly manifested when I returned to PS 139 in Rego Park, as I was about three months ahead of my regular class. Everything they were learning I had already studied.

My "South Beach" experience at the now iconic Drake, continued for two more years until my dad upgraded us to the Raleigh Hotel on Collins Ave and 18th St. which was definitely a "step up" in the Miami hotel hierarchy. Back then, the higher the street on Collins Ave., the fancier the hotel.

However, I was no longer enrolled in private school, but rather my mother, after consulting with my public school teachers, brought with her all my school books, and I had to spend about two hours each day studying and doing my home work under her watchful eyes. I guess you could say I was being "home schooled" before the modern version of it began in the early 1970's.

By then we were no longer taking the Silver Meteor as my dad, an adventurer himself, had us booked on National Airlines for the seven hour flight from LGA which made at least three refueling stops en route.

We returned to the Raleigh once more before "moving uptown" again to the 50's and the Versailles which at the time was a very upscale hotel. Actually, my dad had rented a two bedroom Versailles apartment across the street from the hotel, but as it was a hotel property, we were entitled to all the amenities and benefits of being a hotel guest.

I was now twelve and by then had become an avid swimmer and diver under my dad's tutelage. Upon reflection, I believe I can trace my fascination of the water to those pre teen Florida years.

I thought my Miami experience would last forever, but since I was about to enter Jr. high school our annual two month winter trips to Miami came to an abrupt halt.

I reminisce now and find it very ironic that in 1956, at the age of twenty, I and three of my Clark fraternity brothers (Paul of course included) drove my 1955 two door Chevrolet Bel Air to Miami for our Xmas break and we ended up staying at the Drake Hotel. What goes around comes around.

While enjoying my South Beach experiences in the winter, I was privileged to spend my summers at camp KenMont in Kent Connecticut. The camp was established in 1924 and still exits today, but of course under new directors.

As best I can remember, I was "shipped off" to sleep away camp at the tender age of seven in 1943 and for the first few weeks I was miserable and pleaded to "come home." My parents said they would pack me up and take me home when they came up for visiting weekend. Two weeks later they arrived and when asked if I was ready to come home, replied "are you crazy, I love this place." Naturally, I had become intensely involved in all the athletics including my favorite of swimming and was a "full fledged" camper having a ball.

A few days after they left I woke up in the middle of the night and realized that I had "wet the bed" and my jockey shorts were soaked from the incidence. I had no idea how to hide my embarrassment except to get up in the pitch black, take off my underpants, climb down the bungalow steps, and roll the jockeys into a tight ball and fling them as hard as I could into the woods.

The following morning when we all lined up before breakfast facing the bungalow, I and everyone in the bunk, noticed something white on the roof. When the shorts were retrieved they were promptly handed to me as of course my name was expertly sewn into the waist band so there was no denying my ownership. What an embarrassing feeling for a seven year old, but my bunk mates were understanding as they too had similar occurrences, but were just smart enough to place the shorts into the bottom of their laundry bags. How stupid of me, in my moment of panic, to have thought I could reach the woods with my soiled evidence.

Two weeks later at a flag raising ceremony with all of the campers standing around the flagpole, the director, Dr. Kiviat called out the name of one of my buddies and asked him to come up and stand by his side. We all thought he was getting an award so when my name was then called out I was elated that I was probably going to be recognized for my athletic accomplishments the preceding few weeks.

When I was standing on the other side of the director, he had us both turn around and with the use of a megaphone, he announced that if he found any other campers who were so dirty around the neck and ears, he would immediately fire the counselors who's bunk those campers came from.

Shit, no one told me I had to shower every day, and how the hell was I supposed to see behind my neck and ears? Two weeks and two humiliations, and yet I managed to hang in and enjoy every moment of my camping experience to the extent that I opted for the "post camp week" when most of the other campers went home.

The following year, 1944, I became enthralled with horseback riding to the point that I requested that I be allowed to spend every day at the stables, cleaning out the stalls, and assisting with the horses. After receiving a special dispensation from the camp director (and my parents of course) I ended up spending every day there which afforded me the opportunity to ride almost non stop. In a few weeks I was allowed to gallop and jump and I was in all my glory as an equestrian who had learned to ride English, Western and Military style.

As fate would have it, in mid summer of 1944 there was a massive polio epidemic and most camps including KenMont, closed down about half way thru the season, and unfortunately that was the end of my sleep away camping experience.

From then on it was Rockaway, Atlantic Beach or Long Beach in that order.

CITIES AND COUNTRIES VISITED 1971 – 2010

I have continuously professed that although my career afforded us a comfortable life style, it was the extensive travel that was the most meaningful part of my business and personal life. Laura and I were so fortunate to be able to gallivant so extensively for twenty five years, bonding along the way and being exposed to various cultures and culture itself. We loved it and so did Blair and Brie.

International Cities and frequency of visits

Acapulco, Amalfi, Arezzo, Athens, Bangkok (2), Basle(2), Bermuda, Bologna, Bombay. Cannes (2), Canton (Kwangchow (6), Capri(2), Cap Antibes(2), Casserta (6), Cebu City, Corsica, Deauville, Delhi(2), Dubrovnik, Durazzano (6), Dusseldorf (2), Elba, Frankfurt (2), Florence, Fleur., Geneva, Hamburg (4), Hong Kong(24), Ibiza, Idar Oberstein(2), Istanbul, Ischia, Kaufburen, Kusadasi, Kyoto(2), Lake Como, Lausanne. Lisbon, Lucerne, London (6), Manila, Madrid (6), Marseilles, Media de Sorrento, Mexico City, Milan (10), Montreal, Munich, Nassau & the Bahamas, Naples (3), Nice(2), Osaka (3) Paris (24), Peking
(Beijing), Positano, Puerto Vallarta, Prague, Puerto Ercole, Reims, Rhodes, Rio de Janero, Rome (2), San Jose (3), St. Moritz, St. Tropez, Salzburg,, Stuttgart, Taipei (6), Tokyo (8), Toronto (3), Torre Del Greco (6), Venice(2), Vienna, & Zurich :

Countries visited

Austria, Brazil, Canada, Checkoslavika, Costa Rica, England, France, Germany, Greece, Hong Kong, India, Italy, Japan, Mexico, Peoples Republic of China, Philippines, Portugal, Spain, Switzerland, Taiwan, Thailand, Turkey, & Yugoslavia.

In addition to our international travel, we did pretty well in the States as well, either at personal appearances I was making or when we visited our area showrooms or on vacations. Again a very rewarding and educational experience

Cities and states visited in U.S A.

Albuquerque, Santa Fe and Taos, New Mexico, Alconquitt and Portland Maine, Aspen, Durango, Denver, and Telluride, Colorado, Atlanta, Georgia, Boca Raton, Miami, Ft. Lauderdale, Marathon, Palm Beach, Orlando, and Tampa St. Petersburg, Florida, Boston, Cape Cod (Hyannis port, Martha's Vineyard and Nantucket) Massachusetts, Chicago, Illinois, Dallas, Houston, and San Antonio, Texas,

Des Moines, Iowa,   Kansas City, and St. Louis Missouri,, Los Angeles, Newport, San Francisco, and San Diego California, New Orleans, Louisiana, Newport, and Providence Rhode Island, Salt Lake City, Utah, Seattle, and Portland Washington. Helena, Wyoming, Reno and Las Vegas, Nevada, Bethesda, Maryland and Washington D.C, Philadelphia, Lewisburg and Media Pennsylvania.

Islands visited

It was not all business travel, as we did vacation as well in
Bermuda, Capri, Corsica, Elba, Eleuthera, Ibiza, Ischia, Mykonos, Nassau, Rhodes, Santorini, Sardinia, Sicily:

MY FINAL WORDS TO LAURA - 2010

Laura and I both experienced the unpleasant task of burying our parents and so it was that we discussed the inevitability of one of us passing as we wanted it to be clearly defined as to how we desired our respective demises to be observed.

My mom and dad had never made any appropriate funeral or burial arrangements, but I had available burial sites at Mt. Ararat in Farmingdale, L.I. where I had purchased eight burial plots when Marc had his accident. Laura's folks, wisely, had made arrangements to be interred in Gate of Heaven cemetery in Valhalla N.Y.

Laura made it clear that in the event of her death, she did not want a traditional funeral, but rather a private memorial service to be attended only by family and close friends. She insisted that she did not want to be eulogized by any rabbi or clergyman that had never even met her and she requested that after her cremation, that I preside at the memorial and deliver a short but meaningful eulogy and place her ashes in the "sleeve" she had purchased adjacent to her dad and across from her mom.

And so it was in early May of 2010 about a week after her untimely death that a small group of family and friends motored up to Gate of Heaven and I tearfully managed to utter the following words...

My dearest Laura,

For over forty years we talked, cried, and laughed together and sometimes argued and then hugged tightly, and I feel blessed that we walked this life together and participated in so many exciting experiences and projects as we shared each others joys and sorrows.

You were the ultimate care giver—always putting everyone else's needs before your own and your caring nature was always obvious to us all.

You were the consummate whirling dervish, balancing more projects and deeds at the same time than most people could ever understand.

You were the quintessential creative idea person, possessing more strategic maneuvers than naval intelligence, which made our life together both provocative and challenging, but certainly never mundane.

You served your patients, friends, and country with dignity and honor and we are all gathered here today to salute you for your devotion and dedication to your causes, whatever they may have been. Your impact on the people you touched was always profound. You were truly a unique and very special person imbuing your spirit to all you met, and your absence will be glaring to everyone who knew you.

In our marriage, you were the wind billowing our sails, and I was the anchor, and now with great sorrow, it is time for me to disengage the anchor line, and say "anchors away my love, anchors away."

May that same wind be forever at your back and may the sun shine warm upon your face, and may rain droplets always fall gently upon you.

You were a loving daughter, wife, mother and grandmother, and I can only promise you that to the exclusion of all others, I will dedicate my self to caring for and protecting our children and grand children for the rest of my life, as you would have done.

Thank you for being my wife and best friend and may you finally enjoy the serenity you so justly deserve. Rest in peace my love as you remain in our hearts and minds forever. I will miss you dearly and until we meet again may God hold you in the hollow of his palm.

I loved you with all my heart and I know God will too.

May he bless you forever. Arreviderci & Amen

After the eulogy, taps was played and the small military naval honor guard, adorned in dress whites, presented me with the traditional folded American flag with expressed gratitude from the President and the American people. I must say it was an emotionally charged presentation that left everyone a little teary eyed.

THE LAST QUADRANT   2010-???????

I am not certain what has motivated me to commit all of these life experiences into book form. I hazard the guess that it was an emotional release allowing me to relive, to a certain extent, what I had already experienced and wanting my friends, children and grandchildren to share it with me. At times, I found myself crying or laughing, astonished by my ability to recall events in detail that have not been in my conscious thought for over seventy years, but of course I have no recollection of what I had for breakfast today.

Upon returning home from Bollywood, in December of 2010, as just a "regular guy" with no TV credits to my name, I determined it was appropriate for me to ask my friends to introduce me to some ladies as I knew I was still alive and would shortly be seeking some level of female companionship. Hence, over the last three years, I have dated numerous women, creating meaningful relationships with but a few, as true chemistry is hard to find, and I am ruled first by my heart and instincts, and then by my mind.

I find it charming that I have established a rapport with five single ladies these last three years, yet have not bonded with any new single males, so counting Paul, my best friend of sixty years, my lady friends outnumber the men, five to one, and I would like to pay special thanks to these unattached females that I have interacted with on various levels.

Casey Phelan, a master hair colorist in her own right, shared a close relationship with Laura for almost twenty years. She was Laura's only choice for bartender at all of our festive holiday parties since she possessed not only the necessary bartending skills, but exhibited an uncanny ability to comfortably mingle with all of our guests. Suffice it to say, Laura planned all her soirees based on Casey's availability. Immediately after Laura's passing, Casey and I grieved together, as not only did I lose a spouse, but she lost a dear friend. After being exposed to the full extent of her intellect, I am gratified to say, I convinced her to return to night school to obtain a college degree, and as of this writing she is currently a straight A student. Laura would have definitely approved and been particularly proud of that.

Roberta Leibson, now a Florida resident, was a highly respected sales professional in Les Bernard's New York showroom for over fifteen years. She also accompanied me on two occasions to Paris, to the Bijhorca and Premier Class shows. She has managed to keep in touch every week since Laura passed and has offered me a great deal of humorous sage advice for my "single status." As I entered the senior dating scene, being able to view situations from a woman's vantage point, has been enormously helpful. (?)

Catherine McGillicudy, an old acquaintance, formerly of Brookville and now living in Roslyn, is a charming, witty, cultured French lady and antique specialist. Her son, Patrick was Blair's classmate at Friends Academy those many years ago. We became re acquainted after both Laura and her husband Dan passed just a few months apart. She is one of those rare, genuine, warm, and sincere people I have had the pleasure of meeting and getting to know during my lifetime, and we have shared some fun times together.

Michele Schoenfeld, a Clark alumnus, widowed from a fraternity bother, and now the District Clerk for the White Plains School System, has kept me smiling at least three times weekly with very newsy and lengthy e mails all of which required detailed, thought provoking, time consuming, responses, and to boot she has treated me to multiple lovely lunches at her Westchester country club. Having some professional experience, she graciously volunteered to edit this book, but I opted to bear full responsibility.

Joyce Bernstein, an accomplished NYC residential real estate salesperson, is the only "new" female that I have been introduced to since Laura's passing that I developed a warmhearted relationship with. She is a true lady, single mother, and grandmother, who at times has shared some of her wisdom enabling me to sort things out when my socializing seemed a little perplexing. Joyce was calm and composed enough to call 911 one evening after dinner, and arrange for an ambulance and accompanied me to NY-Presbyterian's emergency room as my pressure had fallen precipitously from a little too much to drink and smoke. Both she and the doctors were amazed that in my seventy six years it was my very first hospital visit...
AS A PATIENT.

Hopefully, I will be able to remain friends with these ladies as they are all "class acts," compassionate, understanding, intelligent, and easy to communicate with.

Paul Shapiro, my only single male friend: Our association has entered its 60th year as we go back to our freshman year at Clark in 1953. Our relationship has never wavered in spite of geographical distance or marital status, and to this day we both rely on each other's opinions before making any crucial decision. As my dad said many years ago, if you have one really good friend in your life time you are a lucky person. Paul and I have been extremely lucky.

To anyone that has chosen to discuss my relationships, I have been very transparent about not wishing to be married again, nor even open to a 24/7 connection. I had been wed for just shy of 50 years between my two marriages, and it is now time for me to enjoy a hiatus. I am not currently seeking a soul mate, but rather a ship-mate/playmate, to sail and travel with, to talk to, and "walk on the beach with," while enjoying some of life's simple pleasures. I question both if and when I will be emotionally prepared to enter into a relationship that will require me to once again assume the obligations and responsibility of being more considerate of some one else's feelings ahead of my own. I am told my attitude about this will evolve over time, so I remain flexible.

A year after Laura's demise I determined that I wished to spend the rest of my life overlooking the water, so I proceeded to purchase a two bedroom ocean front condominium in Long Beach which is now fully furnished and awaiting me to move in which hopefully will occur when I sell my North Shore home. The apartment and its view was so appealing that it caused me to violate my rule of not buying a new residence until the old one is sold, but it was the "last of its kind" in this new building and I bit the bullet and that was almost two years ago. Who knew it would take me so long to sell Muttontown!!!

As I was finishing this book, hurricane Sandy paid us a nasty visit on Long Island which certainly complicated both my social and family life. We were out of power for two weeks and I and my daughters took refuge wherever any of us could find a comfortable place to stay.

Brie and her family initially went to stay at her friend's apartment in Boston, and then after returning to Long Island, they moved in with her in laws as they regained power, and Blair flew down to North Carolina to stay with a gentleman she had been dating.

Having them both out of harms way, I with my pure bred *Coconut Retriever*, Cece, accepted shelter at Catherine's Roslyn apartment where there was no power outage. It was an extremely stressful circumstance for everyone, and in my case, being close to the house enabled me to return every day to feed my cat and check on conditions while keeping my gas usage to a bare minimum, while enjoying the luxury of electricity, heat and hot water. I will always be thankful for her gracious hospitality under difficult circumstances.

Over a fifty four year period, while raising, educating and supporting two families, I have managed to survive the loss of my son, the stress of a messy divorce, multiple custody hearings, estrangement from my two older daughters, the Enron debacle, and the shocking loss of my exceptional partner of some forty years.

Hopefully it is my time to enjoy the last quadrant of my life as I remain healthy in mind (?), body, and spirit, seeking peace and contentment, and vowing to laugh every day.

For the moment, I am just taking one day at a time and will follow the road that unwinds for me as there is no viable option.

Stay tuned!! My life's adventure is not over yet….. I hope!

PERSONAL RECOGNITONS

In addition to previously mentioned family, friends and employees, I choose to mention four other people, that through my business, had a significant impact on my life

TWO LES BERNARD LUMINARIES

Joan George: Our first receptionist at Les Bernard who eventually became my valued administrative assistant. Her logistical and scheduling skills were instrumental in keeping me "on track" in the daily frenzied world of upscale fashion as she radiated an air of true professionalism. More significantly, when she left to form her own advertising agency, Joan was responsible for creating Les Bernard's very unique full page color advertising campaign in Vogue, Harpers, & Elle, and for coining our memorable retail tag line.

"We select what we offer as carefully as you select what you buy"

Jack Patterson: Our prolific Mid West sales representative from 1971 to 1983 whose New England background brought a down home sales approach to the otherwise haughty fashion business. Jack came to Les Bernard from a Massachusetts based silver company and immediately bonded with both me and my dad. In addition to selling the large well known retailers, Jack succeeded in introducing Les Bernard into hundreds of small upscale boutiques in almost every town or city that had more than one traffic light. When asked what made him so successful in this regard, he confided that when he headed in to a town he made a B line for the local luncheonette and befriended the waitress. He told her he was a traveling man and that he wanted to buy a gift for his wife, and could she please direct him to the best dress shop in town. Voila, fifteen minutes later he was at the front door of an upscale boutique, and in almost every instance they became loyal Les Bernard customers.

Amazingly, some thirty years later, though separated geographically, Jack and I still communicate as we have a deep seated mutual respect for each other and we can both be proud that after an initial handshake, and for the twelve years thereafter, we never had anything written about our arrangement …. Try that in today's world!!!!

He was Laura's favorite at Les Bernard…And that says it all.

TWO WELL KNOWN RETAILERS

<u>Andrew Goodman</u>: The son of the founder of Bergdorf Goodman was highly respectful of my dad and his former firm, Vogue Jewelry. And so it was in the early fall of 1964 that Bergdorf Goodman was the first retailer to advertise Les Bernard. Those first two ads on moveable flower pins and "twilight blue pearls" were responsible for instantly elevating Les Bernard to an elite level of recognition in the world of upscale fashion jewelry, a position that I am proud to say, we maintained for some twenty seven years.

I distinctly remember Mr. Goodman sitting me down in his penthouse office atop the store and saying to me and I quote.

"Bernard, you are about to start a long and successful career in the fashion jewelry business, and I caution you that as you ascend the ladder of success there will be those that either work for you, sell to you, buy from you, or socially interact with you, that will be less than honest in their dealings with you. Know it, absorb it, and try to understand it ... but."

"NEVER LET THEM KNOW THAT YOU KNOW"

<u>Stanley Marcus</u> : The son of one of the founders of Neiman Marcus whose fashion jewelry buyer gave Les Bernard it's very first order before we even had samples, an order book, or printed invoices. It was only $300 and basically just a symbolic gesture, but it marked the beginning of a very long and mutually rewarding relationship that lasted some twenty seven years as Neiman's was always one of our largest and most prestigious customers. Mr. Stanley, as he was known in the store, went on to write a number of books one of which was *The Quest for the Best*, which emphasized how important quality was in every aspect of life, so when he chose Les Bernard to create individual jewelry pieces out of artifacts he had gathered from around the world we took it as a supreme compliment. His letters to me are highlighted in my scrap book. His lesson to me: .....

"NEVER SETTLE FOR LESS THAN THE BEST"

PREVIOUSLY PUBLISHED BOOKS

DOING THE RIGHT THING —   EVERY TIME!!!!
By Bernard Shapiro

First published in 2012

consisting of 49 pages of quotes, sayings and caveats

First printing	60 copies
Given to friends And family	58 copies
Kept for posterity	2 copies
Retail price: $ 19.00	total sales not yet fully calculated

ALL THAT I KNOW ABOUT THE DESIGN, MANUFACTURING AND MARKETING OF UPSCALE FASHION JEWELRY.
By Bernard Shapiro

First published in 1980

consisting of 100 blank pages

First Printing	1 copy
Stolen from Les Bernard showroom	1 copy
Retail price: Priceless	considered a rare edition.

IN CONCLUSION

*IF YOU TAKE YOURSELF
AND LIFE TOO SERIOUSLY,*

*YOU WILL FIND IT
IMPOSSIBLE TO LAUGH.*

CPSIA information can be obtained at www.ICGtesting.com
Printed in the USA
BVOW101642050513

319866BV00001B/1/P